# Advance Praise for
## *The Peanut Butter Promise*

"There's no other book that I have read, since The Lord called me into the media mission field thirty years ago, that touches on all of the themes necessary to fulfill the meaningful unique God-given purpose for each of us using our individual talents, abilities, and giftings. *The Peanut Butter Promise* is a field manual for discovering your purpose and achieving your dreams."

**—Michael Van Dyck, Founder, Inspired Entertainment, Los Angeles, CA**

"I have worked with the Roses and their enthusiasm is contagious. Their desire to help others is genuine. *The Peanut Butter Promise* is a hope-filled reminder that each of us is here for a reason. By using our unique gifts to help others, we can find meaning and joy in a troubled world."

**—Pam Jessen, Operations Director, WBAY-TV**

"I've known Steve for a long time. He never gives up and excels in having a positive attitude. *The Peanut Butter Promise* book personifies this and is a must read for those looking to achieve with purpose."

**—Rollie Stephenson, CEO Emeritus, Faith Technologies**

"I love the ability of sports to show people they can achieve things maybe even they thought weren't possible. I love the positive aspects brought out in the training and competition, and *The Peanut Butter Promise* delivers on that. Well done, Steve and Charlene Rose!"

**—Lance Allan,**
**WTMJ Main Sports Anchor and Two-Time**
**Wisconsin "Sportscaster of the Year"**

"I've known Steve for nearly fourteen years. His passion and perseverance is remarkable. *The Peanut Butter Promise* offers transformative lessons in life. It's an inspiring work that can make a difference."

**—Justin Pierce,**
**Media Consultant, Los Angeles, CA**

"If you've lost faith in a world that seemingly bombards you with negativity, you owe it to yourself to read *The Peanut Butter Promise*. You have control over your destiny. This book will help you learn how to seize it."

**—Gary D'Amato, Three-time**
**Wisconsin "Sportswriter of the Year"**

"Simply put, you will not meet two more genuine and caring people than Steve and Charlene Rose. I pray that along with me you'll catch the message of hope, help, and encouragement they have woven deeply into *The Peanut Butter Promise*."

**—Dr. Larry Pesch, Executive Director**
**of Advancement Brookfield Academy**

"The passion and sincerity that Steve and Charlene Rose share to inspire people and to help each of us fulfill our purpose is incredible. Our YMCA family is extremely proud to support the real life lessons and experiences contained in *The Peanut Butter Promise*."

**—Bill Breider, President and**
**CEO, YMCA of the Fox Cities**

"I'm proud to call Steve and Charlene my friends. When I'm around them, their infectious optimism always gives me a refreshing new perspective. The timing for the faith-building message of *The Peanut Butter Promise* couldn't be better. I highly recommend this book."

**—Simran A. Singh of Singh, Singh &**
**Trauben Law, LLP, Beverly Hills, CA**

"Steve and Charlene Rose are both passionate about knowing what God's Word says, but even more passionate about doing the best they can to live out its truths and share its promises. *The Peanut Butter Promise* will help guide you down the path to fulfilling your God-given purpose in this life."

**—Sue Stoddart, Ph.D., Professor**
**Emeritus, Marian University**

"Today, more than ever, we need positive and encouraging things in our lives. Steve and Charlene Rose offer practical ideas that can help all of us in *The Peanut Butter Promise*."

**—Dennis Krause,**
**Green Bay Packers Radio Network**

"In *The Peanut Butter Promise,* Steve shows by example that perseverance and persistence are the winning formula of a life well lived! Read on, and get ready to experience the change you want in your life!"

—**Steve Autey, Marketing Executive, Minneapolis, MN**

"If you're looking for a heartwarming, uplifting, positive experience, Steve Rose provides it with *The Peanut Butter Promise.* He has brought comfort and promise into public view before, and, thankfully, he's at it again."

—**Michael Bauman, former Sports columnist at the Milwaukee Journal and National Columnist at MLB.com**

"Steve and Charlene Rose are the type of people that once you meet them, you feel like you've known them for a long time. I had the opportunity to speak at one of their *Peanut Butter Promise* events, and got to feel firsthand their warmth and sincerity. This is a wonderful book."

—**Craig Culver, Co-founder Culver's**

"Most people read because they love to learn. We learn the most when a book has five important qualities: 1. authentic author 2. meaningful stories 3. easy to read 4. humor 5. sound advice. *The Peanut Butter Promise* has them all! Steve Rose shares from the heart what he learned on the rocky road of life, and he has much to teach us."

—**Hal Urban, author of *Life's Greatest Lessons* and *The Power of Good News***

"Steve and Charlene are two of the most dedicated people I have ever met. Their vision is based on life's experiences, both in business and beyond. They give *The Peanut Butter Promise* its breath and definition."

**—Wayne Larrivee, Green Bay Packers Radio Network**

"Steve Rose's fast-moving and inspiring book *The Peanut Butter Promise* is loaded with great ideas that you can apply immediately to set and achieve all your DreamGoals."

**—Brian Tracy, Author/Speaker**
***Maximum Achievement***

"Steve has provided a compass for all of us with his inspirational writing that guides and fulfills. His passion and character embrace all he touches. I am so thankful for his work and dedication to help so unselfishly with the gifts he provides in *The Peanut Butter Promise*."

**—Kevin Harlan, Announcer,**
**NFL on CBS, NBA, on TNT**

"I have had the privilege to meet and work with Steve Rose over the years, and I have always been very impressed with his heart and his passion to inspire others. He is a very creative person who knows how to engage others in ways that encourage and build them up. The timing of his work, *The Peanut Butter Promise*, could not be better as we live in a world where the need to encourage and inspire others has never been more needed."

**—Jay Zollar, General Manager,**
**WLUK FOX 11 / WCWF CW 14**

"The best compliment I can give any book is that with each page I look forward to reading more. Steve Rose does that with his book *The Peanut Butter Promise*. Steve's style of informal storytelling kept my interest throughout, and his book is full of encouragement and inspiration for today's world."

—**Bill Grady, Star Communications**

"It is interesting how people enter our lives at different times for different reasons and make different impacts. I met Steve a number of years ago and have always been impressed with how he brings his projects to life. His mixture of passion and perseverance is rare, and *The Peanut Butter Promise* is another shining example of his legacy."

—**Dean Leisgang, Award-Winning Journalist/Filmmaker**

"I've known Steve for some time, and the positive impact of his work. *The Peanut Butter Promise* is for anyone who is serious about fulfilling the purpose for their life."

—**Dick Bennett, Coach, Wisconsin Badgers Basketball, NCAA 2000 Final Four**

"Steve's uplifting story of tenacity, second chances, motivation, and much more resonated with my sales team. *The Peanut Butter Promise* is a homerun! It is all-encompassing, touching all aspects of your life. Take back control of your life by putting *The Peanut Butter Promise* into action!"

—**Francis Costello, President and CEO Postal Source**

"What strikes me about the enthusiastically written *The Peanut Butter Promise* is Steve's use of a 7x7 format. He's written seven chapters, each respectively providing reading, and applying one per day for seven weeks provides a small dose of daily refreshment rich in encouragement. The wiser approach is to read one per day, seven times per day, to make it stick like peanut butter so you can realize your true promise."

—**Kevin McCarthy, Author,**
*The On-Purpose Person:*
*Making Your Life Make Sense*

"I'm proud to work with my friends Steve and Charlene during their powerful Peanut Butter Promise events. This book can help anyone, especially those who need hope to believe that they can still succeed and fulfill their purpose after having made many mistakes."

—**Chester Marcol, Professional Addictions Counselor, 1972 NFL Rookie of the Year**

"I've worked with Steve and am amazed how he can take common, everyday occurrences and shine the light on them! Things happen for a reason, and Steve has a talent for showing people why, and *The Peanut Butter Promise* does that too."

—**Dayton Kane,**
**Producer, Peanut Butter Promise Power-Encouragement Podcast**

"God gives us all unique gifts and talents that he wants us to use to fulfill our unique purpose in life. *The Peanut Butter Promise* can help you discover yours, confirm yours, or perhaps give you the desire and hope you need to find yours and live a more fulfilled, blessed, and abundant life. There is a lot of wisdom in this book, and a great read for everyone."

**—John Schiek, Owner, Schiek Sports**

"Steve and Charlene are passionate, humble, and dedicated people with a wonderful message for all of us, especially our youth. Through *The Peanut Butter Promise* they have a special way to make all of us feel better about ourselves and to understand our dreams and desires."

**—Mark J. McGinnis, Circuit Court**
**Judge, Outagamie County, Wisconsin**

"Steve and Charlene Rose are visionaries, loving people who see the deep meaning in life's everyday moments. God bless them for their life's mission and for writing *The Peanut Butter Promise,* which will help many people fulfill their purpose."

**—Rob Riedl, President, Endowment**
**Wealth Management**

"I first became familiar with author Steve Rose through his *Leap of Faith* series of books featuring the spiritual lives of famous Green Bay Packer football players. He has always supported, developed, and championed the faith of others, and now it's *your* turn!"

**—Michael O. Sajbel, Motion**
**Picture Writer and Director**

# THE
# PEANUT BUTTER
# PROMISE

*Spreading Hope to Fulfill Your Purpose!*

# STEVE ROSE

SAVIO
REPVBLIC

A SAVIO REPUBLIC BOOK
An Imprint of Post Hill Press
ISBN: 978-1-64293-774-9
ISBN (eBook): 978-1-64293-775-6

The Peanut Butter Promise:
Spreading Hope to Fulfill Your Purpose!
© 2021 by Steve Rose
All Rights Reserved

posthillpress.com
New York • Nashville

Published in the United States of America
1 2 3 4 5 6 7 8 9 10

This book is dedicated to our parents, Jean and David Rose. Mom, you are a living, unspoken example of unconditional love. Dad, you were the greatest example of the power of having DreamGoals, and passionately pursuing them. Charlene and I love both of you more than words can say.

# CONTENTS

# FOREWORD

When you meet Charlene and Steve Rose, you feel like you've known them for a long time. That's the type of people they are. I've had the opportunity to speak at their Peanut Butter Promise events and have gotten to feel firsthand their warmth and sincerity. Just like their events, I believe this book can help those who will accept its valuable and time-tested message of hope and encouragement. Like the Roses, I believe we each have a special purpose to fulfill throughout our life. So when they asked me if I would write the foreword for this book, I agreed because my story and my family's story agrees with many aspects of the philosophy of the Peanut Butter Promise.

I started in the restaurant business when I was eleven years old, when my parents bought a little A&W drive-in restaurant in the small community of Sauk City, Wisconsin, never dreaming the restaurant industry would become my life's work. Here I am today, at seventy years of age, with fifty-nine years of restaurant experience behind me that started with that drive-in.

Like many young people growing up in the business, I watched my parents work very long hours, seven days a week. I was certain I didn't want to be like them. Well, come to find out, I'm very much like my parents, and I'm lucky for it. You see, my parents taught me so many wonderful things. Yes, they were tough on my brother, sister, and me, but there was always love behind everything they said and did.

They taught us that hard work and long hours would pay off as long as we had passion for our work and the people around us, and the Peanut Butter Promise believes that too. My brother, sister, and I have been blessed in many ways in life, but I believe our greatest blessing is the blessing of love—love of family, love of the people we surround ourselves with, and the love of making a difference for the better in others' lives. Mom and Dad taught us well! If any of what I said in these couple of paragraphs rings true with you, *The Peanut Butter Promise* will be right up your alley!

—Craig Culver, Co-Founder, Culver's

# THE PEANUT BUTTER PROMISE IS FOR YOU

I have good news for you. There's an incredible plan and an exciting purpose for your life. It includes becoming the person you were meant to become, doing things only you can do, and completing assignments only you can complete. Make no mistake about it; you're needed. You're essential. If you came to grips with the potential of the positive impact you can have on your fellow man, it may astound you. You're an original, not a copy; you can never be replicated or replaced.

Of the approximately 7.7 billion people currently inhabiting the earth, there's only ever been, and will only ever be, one person exactly like you! You're different, and I mean that in a good way. You, friend, are one of a kind; your physical appearance, DNA, voice, fingerprints, the desire and dreams in your heart, your favorite color, food, movie, television show, song, or sports team, along with all the activities and hobbies you enjoy make a strong case for this to be true.

I've come to believe that everything has been created for a reason (except maybe the mosquito). We don't always know what the reason for everything is, but not knowing everything keeps us humble, right? That reminds me of a classified ad I once saw in the paper that read:

*Encyclopedias for Sale—My Husband Knows Everything*

Nobody likes someone who knows everything; as a matter of fact, the people who *think* they do bother the daylights out of people like me, who *do*. Just kidding. Truth be known, I'm on a comeback, and it may very well take eternity to complete it. I may not ever "arrive," but I have "left." I do confess that, among many other things, I am a recovering "know-it-all." The Peanut Butter Promise philosophy can't emphasize enough that you've been designed for significance. You matter, and it doesn't matter that you don't know everything, but it's crucial to do everything to fulfill your purpose. It goes as far as saying you have a deep obligation to do so. You're a necessary piece of the world and, quite possibly, a much bigger one than you may think.

The vision for the philosophy of the Peanut Butter Promise came to me in 2007. I received a call from Justin Pierce from Los Angeles, and from that conversation came a vivid and deep revelation that although I had a unique purpose to fulfill, I needed others to help me fulfill it. This is where the metaphor of peanut butter needing jelly to make a great sandwich came to mind. Jelly on bread alone tastes good, but adding peanut butter made a great sandwich.

With all of this in mind, here is the Peanut Butter Promise. It is a hope-and-encouragement-filled, priorities-based, and integrity-centered life-enhancing philosophy that professes that, "We're each born with every talent, ability, gift, and the necessary desire to fulfill a meaningful and unique God-given purpose. Just as peanut butter was destined to find jelly and make a great sandwich, Peanut Butter Promise Partners come into our lives to help us achieve our DreamGoals and fulfill our purpose. The dreams and desires of our heart—those that are in agreement with our purpose—are meant to come true at the right time."

Let's break this down. I have said the Peanut Butter Promise provides the assurance that "We're each born with every talent, ability, and gift, and the necessary desire to fulfill a meaningful and unique God-given purpose." The fact that you are unique and one of a kind means you are competing with no one. You do not need to look left or right, just stay in your lane and answer your calling, which is to discover your purpose and do what you're supposed to do during your time here on Earth. If you don't know your life's purpose, this book will help you.

None of us can fulfill this purpose alone. The Peanut Butter Promise recognizes this: "Just as peanut butter was destined to find jelly to make a great sandwich, Peanut Butter Promise Partners come into our lives to help us achieve our DreamGoals and fulfill our purpose." These are God-sent people, who are either in our life now, or have yet to come into it, who will help us complete our worthy assignments.

Encouragingly, the Peanut Butter Promise declares, "The dreams and desires of our heart—those that are in agreement with our purpose—are meant to come true at the right time." The part that can be a bit frustrating (OK, a lot frustrating) is the part about timing. It's not always easy, but if we will allow patience to become our friend, we'll be amazed what will happen in, and through, our life.

Peanut Butter Promise Players understand that their greatest need is to be loved and accepted, but their greatest fear is to be rejected, so they operate under the Golden Rule, treating others the way they want to be treated. They know true joy and success only come while serving others. One of the miracles of the Peanut Butter Promise is that as it gives, it also receives. But to be clear, it's not about *getting* more, but *becoming* more as a person.

The philosophy also purports that none of us are beyond redemption, restoration, or reconciliation with God, family, friends, foes, coworkers, and the like. The Peanut Butter Promise believes in second, third, even seventy-seven times seventy chances for the truly repentant and sincere; the Peanut Butter Promise's greatest passion is to serve others without provocation, seeking no attention or credit.

It is a one-per-customer program of which membership is free, but the buyer must predetermine the cost they'll pay to have its benefits. It acknowledges that our two greatest personal assets are health and time, and the time for action is not tomorrow or sometime down the road, but now!

The definition of success in the Peanut Butter Promise is: "Keeping our priorities in order and integrity intact as we use our talents, abilities, and gifts to the best of our ability to achieve our DreamGoals and fulfill our purpose." Please read that sentence again. Upon further review, you'll notice that it never refers to a person's social or business status, the size of an investment portfolio, the number of homes one owns, nor does it derive its self-esteem from "likes" on social media or the quantity of followers.

The Peanut Butter Promise believes wholeheartedly that we were not created to be successful, but faithful, to passionately develop a well-thought-out plan of action and persevere until we fulfill our purpose and destiny. Of course, death can mess that up, which is why it is so important to move now if we have our health. If the definition of success above has an element of truth, that would mean you can choose to be successful *now*!

Furthermore, to have peace, joy, and true success as you walk in the power of your purpose, you should not compare yourself to or compete with anyone. To be jealous and envious of another person is a huge insult to yourself. Don't even go there. To get caught up in wanting to be someone else will be an exercise in futility. Stop that—and now. In one of her television messages, world-recognized Bible teacher Joyce Meyer said, "You can't be someone else because they're already taken." Besides, you're one in 7.7 billion, remember? You're special.

You may be thinking, "Well, Steve, I don't feel special, and you see, there's so much you don't know about me, and I've messed up really badly." Oh, really? Let's talk about that; I'll go first. Today, I am living my dreams. I have a wonderful and loving wife, and 77 percent of the time, I am living right in the epicenter of the peace of the Peanut Butter Promise—all this for me after many years of being an alcoholic, going bankrupt, and getting divorced, for starters. Be assured, you are not stuck where you are; you can change yourself by changing your thinking, habits, and associations.

If you're reading this book, and up to this point in your life you have practiced good disciplines, and are currently receiving the benefits that have come from them, that's great. That said, I believe very strongly that the Peanut Butter Promise may be able to provide a few tips to make your life even better. On the other hand, if you are like me and you are looking to get back on track, then keep reading. You have found help, or help has found you! Let not your heart be troubled; things can change for the good—and sooner rather than later.

Now, will this be easy? Nope. Will you still have setbacks, heartbreaks, and have to endure disappointment and some hardships and grief? Yep. That's an inevitable part of life. I love an original quote my wife Charlene came up with in our first podcast when she said, "You may not be in the best place, but you can find the best in that place." Her incredible wisdom is just one of the seventy-seven things I love and adore about her. Truth is we have learned that the bigger the setback and its pain, the greater its potential for good, but it's a process to come to that conclusion.

I hope you will choose to read the next chapter, where I reveal all the dumb, stupid, irresponsible things I did—and that is being kind to myself. But you will also see that through the grace of God, I was able to make a decision on April 15, 1991, that rocked hell and put me on the path to the fulfillment of my Peanut Butter Promise.

It is our most fervent prayer that we will convince you to become a Peanut Butter Promise Player. They are people who get up every day and make a conscious choice to live with a positive and expectant attitude. They are honest, kind, and compassionate. They love self-discipline, they have a personal development plan, they take 100 percent responsibility for their future, know their purpose, and have a clear plan to fulfill it.

While Peanut Butter Promise Players are moving on the path of their purpose, they also lift and help others. They send timely notes of encouragement while the receiver can still read them and send flowers while they can still smell them. They know that one note sent is worth seven in their email drafts.

Peanut Butter Promise Players realize that life is a one-per-customer program, of which membership is without a monetary cost. Charlene and I have learned that nothing that is truly good comes to us free; we must pay full price, and in advance, before we see and taste the fruits of the Peanut Butter Promise, and I'm confident this applies to you as well.

It's our hope that your life has calm, and you are enjoying the fruits of obedience and self-discipline. However, if you are currently in a mess—call today a day of change—make the necessary changes and turn the pages of this book and on your life, not forgetting the past, but learning from it. One of the many lessons Charlene and I have learned and continue to understand more deeply everyday is: "You can't mess up your life badly enough to not have your dreams come true if you repent and get a new and better plan."

Look at us. Charlene was a drug addict and has been healed for nearly forty years. I drank heavily from 1978 to 1991 until I crashed and asked for help, and it got a lot better quickly. Today, we are blessed to be sharing our stories through the Peanut Butter Promise with you or anyone else who may find faith-building hope and encouragement through it. Sure, we have our share of struggles and challenges, but we're also experiencing the peace and prosperity the Peanut Butter Promise has to offer. The good news is you can have them too. But there are guidelines to follow, and the sooner we learn that laws are bridges, not walls—that healthy boundaries are good—the better off we'll be.

Sometimes it takes the fires of affliction—spending time in a furnace—before we realize it's time to make changes. I love the story about a group of women in a Bible study who came upon a remarkable expression in the third verse of Proverbs 17: "And He shall sit as a refiner and purifier of silver." One woman spoke up and said the verse was intended to convey the sanctifying influence of the grace of God. Then, she said she would visit a silversmith and report to the other women what he said on the subject.

She went accordingly and, without telling the object of her errand, begged to know the process of refining silver, which the smith described to her.

"But, sir," she said, "do you sit while the work of refining is going on?"

"Oh, yes, ma'am," replied the silversmith. "I must sit with my eye steadily fixed on the furnace, for if the time necessary for refining is exceeded in the slightest degree, the silver will be injured."

The woman at once saw the beauty and comfort of the expression "He shall sit as a refiner and purifier of silver." God sees it needful to put His children into a furnace. His eye is steadily intent on the work of purifying, and His wisdom and love are both engaged in the best manner for them. Their trials do not come at random; "the very hairs of your head are all numbered." (Luke 12:7)

As the woman was leaving the shop, the silversmith called her back and said he had forgotten to mention that the only way to know when the purifying process is complete is when he can see his own image reflected in the silver. Amen. The Peanut Butter Promise agrees that once we've gone through a little hell, it helps us appreciate heaven more. But to get there, sometimes we need to make some necessary changes. That's just one of the reasons we are writing this, to help you or someone you know do that if necessary. You're not alone.

One day, Charlene and I were glued to watching a rocket ship take off for a daylong journey to the International Space Station. It was mind-blowing; shortly after liftoff, the graphic on television showed that the rocket ship was cruising at a speed of seventeen thousand miles an hour! Our friend Rob Riedl reminded us that the most difficult part of that journey—the liftoff—was the first inch. That's right, the first inch. It is at that time when those fires burn and smoke bellows from underneath that capsule trying to get it off the launching pad. But once they get liftoff, wow. And maybe you're in that place where you need to go just that first inch. If so, do it—and do it now!

Friend, you have so much to give. There is so much in you that can help others. Do you remember jukeboxes of the '50s, '60s, '70s, and '80s? They played music, but you had to insert a quarter into them to draw it out of them. You're a bit like a jukebox in that you still have "music"—dreams and desires—in you. In other words, "Don't die with your music still in you!"

The Peanut Butter Promise guarantees that if you honestly, earnestly, and diligently seek it, it will find you! It is no respecter of persons; it rejoices in those, like me and Charlene, who were once blind and now seek to see, those who were lost and want to be found. Its joys are for you too!

It may take a page or chapter or two for you to catch it, but here are a few ways you will know you've found the Peanut Butter Promise or that it has found you. There will be brightness and vibrancy in your spirit; your heart will feel a sense of hope like never before. You will feel encouraged beyond measure. You'll find the energy and courage to confront many of your issues, and when you do, although it may take some time, you'll be successful in dealing with them.

You'll have a passion for life like never before; you'll have a desire to get up early and run toward the fulfillment of your purpose.

If you can find the courage to go deeper and take a leap of faith with us, just know we're here to help you every step of the way. We mean it.

That's a Peanut Butter Promise.

# CHAPTER 1

# FROM ENTREMANURE TO ENTREPRENEUR

loved growing up on a dairy farm. It was the work I hated. The hours were long, and the cows needed to be milked two times a day, even on holidays—the audacity of them. And in my humble-but-deadly-accurate opinion, the pay wasn't commensurate for the work performed. I did get a different revelation on the issue one day from my father. May I preface this story by pointing out that at seventeen years dumb, your thinking may not be right? In this case, that was me.

This is a true story. Believing full well I was being overworked and underpaid at Rose-E-Vue Farm, I went to my father to present my labor dispute to him personally. With knees shaking, armed with a calculator in one hand and a piece of paper with the number of my meager monthly salary in the other and the alacrity of the great TV attorney Perry Mason, I began my opening statement.

"Dad, I've taken my monthly salary and, with that, have added up the number of hours I'm working per month. After doing the math, it would seem that you're paying me only about seventeen-

and-a-half cents an hour. I think that should be more." I observed that Dad was listening, although not intently, as he pushed the silage cart, forking out servings to the hungry cows.

Now, all great sales professionals will say this is the time when we should shut up and listen. Pop reflected and then looked at me, locking into my pupils, and the explanation that proceeded from his mouth proved, one, he was the boss, and two, he was much more schooled in wage negotiations than me.

"Well, son, you see, your pay is performance-based. Thanks for providing those numbers—the amount of your wages—to me. Based on those figures, I didn't realize it, but you're overpaid. You're fired."

And with that, he coldly and calmly turned around and continued feeding the cows. I, on the other hand, stood stunned at such a quick verdict—practically with head in hands that had dropped the calculator and paper to reflect. In all fairness to me, at seventeen years stupid, one (in this case, me) may fail to calculate their "full benefit package." In my case, this included a blue '68 Chevy Impala that Dad had purchased for me, paid insurance premiums on the car, and an unlimited supply of gasoline, not to mention my room, board, clothing, and many other amenities I'd failed to take into consideration before asking for a raise.

With a fresh revelation on the subject, only a moment later, I yelled, "Pop, can we forget we ever had this conversation?" He nodded. Thank goodness he relented about firing me. From that moment on, I never brought up or complained about wages to my father again. Now, I can tell you we had many laughs over the years about that conversation! We joked to each other that our accountants had been negotiating for years, working toward a settlement, but I dropped it, knowing there was a good chance I'd wind up owing Mom and Dad!

Truth be told, I was the most blessed person on the planet then, and by the grace of God, I still am today. If I could have personally chosen my parents, I would have picked David and Jean Rose, and I thank them for bringing me into this world, making it possible for me to be here today writing this book. I'm the youngest of six children; there's Gloria, Jim, Gary, Dan, Dale, and Steven (that would be me). As the story goes, my brother Dale and Mom wanted a girl instead of me. I was supposed to be little Lori Jean. But they got me. They raised me and the rest of us the best they knew how. Be assured, our family was not, nor will ever be, *The Brady Bunch*.

Gloria is by far my favorite big sister; it matters not that she is my only sister. I love her more than words can express. Jim taught me to play golf, but I still love him anyway. Gary taught me to play Wiffle Ball, which came in handy, helping me win a tourney in 2008. That's true. Dan allowed me to wear his clothes when I was in high school, but best of all, he let me drive his hot blue Nova. He's still a wonderful guy who lives close by. Dale, well, you'll be hearing a lot about him coming up. He's special beyond description, a real impetus behind the message of *The Peanut Butter Promise*.

On Sunday mornings in the '60s, Mom and Dad piled us into the banana-yellow '57 Chevy to go to church. We wore nerdy-looking hats, but they made us stand out, which was great. One morning in 1969, at nine years old, I recall during a church service while the congregation was singing a hymn when in the twinkling of an eye, I recall feeling like God whispered to me, *I have a great plan and purpose for your life, Steve.* From that moment on, I have felt imbued with a deep sense of purpose and destiny, but boy, did I get off course along the way, which is a bit like saying the Titanic had only a leak, but I digress.

In my early years, for the most part, I stayed out of trouble. When I was fourteen, I met my buddy, Keith, who was five years older than me. He was a wonderful guy. Still is. From the time I met him, he possessed a caring heart. He took on a much-needed role to protect me. He still has a great sense of humor. "Kite" kept me out of trouble. We weren't angels by any means; we stayed out too late and slept in church from time to time because we'd been out a little late the night before. One of the many wonderful things about my pal "Kite" was that he had a driver's license, and travel we did, with The Beach Boys, Jim Croce, and Olivia Newton-John blasting from the speakers of his eight-track tape player.

I didn't get great grades at Campbellsport High School—I'd guess maybe a B- average…OK, maybe C+. I could have done better for sure. One good subject I took there was Miss Prahl's typing class, which as a writer has come in handy, but I wish I'd paid more attention in Mr. Vollmer's English class, but if I had, we may not have needed him today to help edit and clean up the manuscript for this book. The fact that he was able to do this forty-four years after having him as my teacher is a thrill. I'm grinning as I write; you can't make this stuff up.

While at CHS, I was an overcompetitive athlete, who, to get attention, sported a huge afro hairdo, which sat on top of a big head and ego that held an overblown opinion of myself. I played basketball for Coach Larry Hilgendorf, baseball for Coach Hubie Diekvoss, and American Legion baseball for Coach Dick Knar. I am grateful for each of those men who helped me, but with a special fondness and deep respect for Larry Hilgendorf. He taught me many valuable life lessons that still benefit me today. Honestly, he is one of the finest men I've ever known.

One of the first tragedies I experienced was the sudden loss of Billy Strassburg. At only sixteen, he was killed in the early morning hours of June 16, 1976, in a car accident. He failed to make a curve and hit a culvert. He was a wonderful person. He was my friend and teammate, the kind of guy who'd give you a silly grin in the hallway and you'd just laugh, knowing it was probably something we'd discussed the day before at practice.

That wake and funeral was awful. I was stunned, and I've never seen so many kids crying in one place. I'll never forget the following season after winning the conference championship in February 1977. Shortly after the game, we playfully held Coach Hilgendorf under the shower before he made a touching remark.

"We know there is one guy we wish was here with us."

In that moment, I finally broke over the loss of Billy.

A pivotal day for me was in the summer of 1977. It was right before my senior year, when my father, who was a passionate student of personal development and growth, took me to a Positive Mental Attitude (PMA) rally. A few of the speakers that day were Paul Harvey, Dr. Robert Schuller, Earl Nightingale, and W. Clement Stone. However, the guy who caught my ears and held my hot fudge-propelled brain and attention-deficit-disordered mind was a dynamic, fast-walking and talking Texan with a southern drawl by the name of Zig Ziglar.

I was so profoundly impressed with his riveting message of faith, hope, and encouragement that I went home and made a decision that I would set a goal to one day publicly deliver a message just like Mr. Ziglar. I became a loyal follower of his philosophy that says, "You can have everything in life you want if you'll just help enough other people get what they want." To me, Zig Ziglar, next to my father, was the most passionate public purveyor of hope, encouragement, and faith to ever walk this planet.

After high school, in May of 1978, despite being overly medicated with beer, I had a successful season playing Legion baseball for Coach Knar, who was majorly responsible for helping me become an all-state third baseman. Family friend Jim Gantner, who was from my hometown, was playing for the Milwaukee Brewers at the time. He sat next to me in the dugout during the All-Star game that was played that summer after a Red Sox versus Brewers game at the old County Stadium in Milwaukee. He let me wear his Brewers helmet while I swung at the first pitch I saw and grounded out to second. We, the South, lost to the North. I think the score was 5–1.

I should have enrolled at a college that had a baseball program. I know I would have been a four-letterman. (All of them would have been home to Mom asking for money.) I was sitting with Coach Knar one day when he had a coach on the phone from a school with a good baseball program. I should have gone there, but I'd become quite attached to the local beer joints, so I decided to go to a local junior college. It was there I learned quickly what I already knew: I didn't like school. So, at the semester's end, I quit. (Spoiler alert: That was a mistake.) But hey, what better time to quit school than when you know it all, right?

I didn't tell the school I was dropping out; I just stopped going, and on the heels of this choice came a series of cataclysmic events that would hit me like a tidal wave, blasting me into a place of pain that I had absolutely no capability to endure. I was enveloped with a deep fear to fail, but even worse, I had a fear to feel. Although beer had not been an issue in high school, my behavior and rotten way of thinking proceeded to overtake me. My potential to *do* or *become* anything in line with my purpose and destiny was heading out the window—and fast.

One light in the midst of that darkness was that I received an internship from a local radio station. Along with a desire to become a motivational speaker, I wanted to become a radio disc jockey. Proving even a blind squirrel can find a few nuts, I was fortunate to be hired by Peanut Butter Promise Partner Jim Zielinski (Felix Templeton on the radio) at WFON in early 1979 to play '60s and '70s music. Doing the Saturday night "Wax Museum" show remains one of the professional highlights of my life.

During the week, I worked many hours on the air from six until midnight, then hit the bars for a quick sixpack, then proceeded to weave home on dark country roads, stumbling into the family farm house around 2 a.m. About 77.7 percent of the time (my percentages), when I arrived at the farm, I was still pretty inebriated. I was not alone; my brother Dale was there sometimes too, in the same condition.

I'd burn my brother and I some hamburgers and boil a can of clam chowder. As I ate, I read Dad's *Success* magazine. It contained articles of inspiration from people like Zig Ziglar, Paul Harvey, Earl Nightingale, W. Clement Stone, and many of the others in the personal development and encouragement arena. There I sat, drunk, totally convinced I could and would one day do the same thing as those guys. And by the grace of God, I did, but not before a lot of self-induced pain and suffering.

In the fall of 1981, my radio career led me to the cornfields of Clarion, Iowa, where I found my first full-time radio work (and I use the word "work" loosely). It was there I met a few wonderful people: Bill Grady, Steve Autey, and Gary Martin. I eventually lost that job and wound up back in Wisconsin, where I took a job at WNAM. Despite a beer-soaked brain, I managed to get good ratings doing the afternoon show, all while pretending to be someone I wasn't. I was a pretty lost soul, basking now in the need for more alcohol, nicotine, and other forms of self-medication. I had a rude awakening on Friday, July 31, 1987.

In the middle of my radio show, I was called into management's office by my boss, Bob, which I knew wasn't good. In the presence of him and the general manager, I was promptly fired for having a bad attitude, insubordination, and a list of other baggage. My sudden dismissal was justified, but I was devastated and in shock. In an act of compassion, they closed the curtains in the office so the others did not have to see me weep. I did appreciate that. Words cannot describe my embarrassment and hurt in that moment. Shortly after the meeting, I packed a box with my headphones and other belongings and was escorted out the door like a prisoner. My sentence was about to begin.

A few days after getting the ax from WNAM, I was on a pretty good self-pity beer binge. One early morning, a few weeks in from the job loss, I was lying in bed with a hangover headache setting in and could feel a warm beam of the morning sunshine covering me through the window of the room. It felt like I was in a zone of being asleep but also quite awake, with a sense of calm that had taken over every part of my being that was indescribable. It was more than the sun that had enveloped me. I couldn't move, but I had no panic and was peacefully paralyzed. For a split second, I thought, *Am I dying?* Then, out of nowhere came a vision. In it, I was lying back in a chair on the lawn of my childhood home. Beside me was my Grandpa Rose (who had died fourteen years prior). We were looking up into the sky, where a puffy cloud formed the words:

## *MAJOR VOICE IN PALM OF HAND*

I had no idea what that meant then, and I can only imagine and interpret it now. What I *do* know is that message brought comfort at the time. It would take another four years before my roof collapsed and I surrendered. It's unfathomable to me today how I chose to remain in the situation I had been in. At the heart of what I was dealing with were alcohol and other addictions (those of the male gender may be able to relate).

I give you a disclaimer: I am *not* a professional addictions counselor, but I've been held in addiction's firm grip. Addiction has *no* integrity—none whatsoever, nada, zilch. It is ruthless and seeks to rob, kill, and destroy the one it inhabits. Not only that, in the same way, addiction mercilessly permeates, perpetuates, and proceeds to rip out the hearts of families and souls in its way and wake. Because it has no integrity, it has no regard for truth, so it lies constantly. There is still hope to escape its grips; I'm living proof of that. Anyone, anywhere, regardless of their circumstance can break through and fulfill their purpose. I've done it, so has my wife Charlene, and if we can do it, so can you, and the Peanut Butter Promise can help.

Unfortunately, hope wouldn't find me for some time yet, or I wouldn't let it in for a couple years after the sunshine in the bedroom experience, but it did find me eventually, after I acknowledged I had hit bottom and asked for and received help for alcoholism and other vices I'd allowed to destroy me. What precipitated my healing was another awful, self-induced radio experience. In 1990, at thirty years old, I decided to enter the great realm of entrepreneurialism, take a shot at the American Dream, and buy a local AM radio station that was for sale. (Spoiler alert: This was a huge mistake. The dream quickly became a nightmare.)

Within just a few months, I was far behind on my bills and other commitments. It was chaos, confusion, and desperation 24/7/365. When the phone rang or when I went to the mailbox, I cringed, not knowing what I was in for. Only a few months after taking charge, I was in such a mess at the station that it became necessary to summon a handful of soon-to-be former employees into my office where I dropped a bomb on them. I had to confess to them that my business plan (or lack of it) had blown up, and that I needed to let them go immediately.

I'll never forget the look of shock on their glum faces, the sadness in their eyes, and having to deal with their feelings of betrayal. To make matters worse, many of them were friends I had invited to join me. Some had even left jobs to do so. I felt like a rat fink. I did feel a bit better adding a few bucks to their last paychecks I handed to them before I went into my office to cry.

Before a pool of tears could gather on the planner on top of my paper-heaped desk, the phone rang. I waited for about seven seconds before I got the guts to answer it. It didn't take long for me to learn that the hits at the radio station kept right on coming.

"Hi, this is Steve," I said like my normal, cheerful self.

"Steve, this is Roy at the bank." He was the vice president. "Say, we have an urgent situation to deal with. About an hour ago, the Department of Revenue levied on your checking account and took every penny you had in there, so you now have a zero balance. We have four of your employees in the lobby who tried to cash their paychecks, and we had to turn them away."

I sat stunned. It was unimaginable how my day could get any worse, but it had. And then, he fired this question.

"What would you like us to tell them?"

That question brought me to a new low. It was surreal. My body temperature felt like it soared to about 117 degrees and a wet blanket of about seventy-seven pounds had been wrapped around my entire body, mind, and spirit. I thought to myself, *Is this really happening, or is this just a nightmare?* Unfortunately, it was a stunningly real and sobering moment. It was one I feared I couldn't get through soberly. That would prove to be right, but back to Roy at the bank. I thought to myself, *So, now what?* Then, I gave him this answer.

"Roy, I'll be right down to deal with this unfortunate situation. I apologize for this. It's certainly not my employees' fault," I told him.

After a slow, twelve-minute trip downtown to the bank, an idea came to me. It wasn't ideal, but necessary. I decided to draw $7,000 from a credit card and deposit it in the payroll account. Incidentally, that card was already nearly maxed-out. I wish I could tell you this was the last time this would happen, but it wasn't. Those wonderful people at the Department of Revenue must have alerted the IRS that we would dump cash into our payroll account the day before our paydays, which were the fifth and twentieth of each month, so they could levy and empty the accounts a short time after they saw funds were there.

The harsh truth I needed to come to grips with was that I'd become a self-centered, uncompassionate, numb, drunken egomaniac with an inferiority complex. And the irony was that, at eighteen, one of the perverted goals I had was to become a "big shot," go regularly to cocktail hour, and "drink my way to success." (Spoiler alert: That didn't work; as a matter of fact, it has never worked for anyone.) The question for those around me who could see what was going on was "When was he going to admit his bottom and ask for help?" That would take a miracle—divine intervention—and I received it, and none too soon.

That day arrived on Monday, April 15, 1991. I awoke, lying flat on my back, staring at the ceiling. It was deathly quiet. I peered over my left shoulder from my waterbed at the clock on the nightstand. It turned to 8:21a.m. The heaviness of the world was pinning me to the bed. My head felt like a football that was going to explode from my self-numbing drinking binge. I'd been in bad places in my life spiritually, emotionally, and mentally, but this time, it was different.

Some of my past attempts to cut back or quit drinking (some at the strong suggestion of family and a few others) were futile, as frustrating as trying to type with boxing gloves on. In retrospect, it was inevitable that if I didn't make a serious change in my behavior, especially where my drinking was concerned, that I was going to crash. Jim Rohn defines inevitability as "being on a raft one hundred yards from Niagara Falls with no oars." This time had been coming for about thirteen years, when at eighteen years and innocent, I took a drink (then the drink took a drink), and now, the drink was taking me. This particular morning was different from that of the thousands of previous hangovers. It seemed as if I was being given a blaring warning from well beyond me. I felt a deep sense that if I persisted in my current behaviors, something terrible was going to happen. In many ways, I lacked the courage to live, but I was also deathly afraid of dying.

It felt like I had one foot on the dock and one on the boat, and the boat was leaving. I knew I needed to do something—make a drastic change—and quickly. It was then that I made a decision that rocked the bowels of hell and made angels in heaven rejoice and cheer. I sat up and said out loud, "I'm an alcoholic, and I need help!" In no time flat, I felt a peace like never before. It felt like a seven-hundred-pound sack had been lifted from me. I called a friend, who contacted a local alcohol treatment center, where my chair was waiting for me the next day.

"Hi, my name is Steve, and I'm an alcoholic," I confessed to a group of other tired and humble souls, who, like me, had been defeated by their demons, mercifully chased into confronting and dealing with their addiction. Deep down inside, I'd hoped for a very long time that I'd end up in this very place, and although I was a tad nervous, I was also immensely grateful. Truth be told, for a great share of time up to that point, I'd been a sucker for a happy ending, hoping I could get the help I needed and then go on to make a positive difference.

I'm still a softy for a happy ending, just ask Charlene as we watch movies while eating bushels of popcorn and sipping on cherry cola on one of our twice-weekly date nights. Miraculously, I've been sober now for thirty years, but don't ask me about Cheetos or a white Long John donut. I'd surely flunk a random test for those, but we have to have some vices, right? Seriously, I thank God every day that He allowed hell to scare the drink out of me, so today, I can guide others to their happy ending if they will choose to do so.

Through my painful process, I learned that those around us who are in pain want hope, real hope, not hype from the mouths of those who spew their sugarcoated quotes and platitudes. These people mean well, but because they really can't relate to us and the pain and suffering we're going through, their statements are hurtful. They add other well-meaning but dumb things like, "You know, when a door closes in a house, there is another one open." Although that may be true, they have no idea that, at that time for us, we are also going through hell in gasoline underwear, running through scorching flames in the hallways to find it.

Again, I get why they say those things, but they have no clue. If you have been or are currently suffering, I get it, and I can tell you that, for me, things are much better today. I'm married to my best friend of six years, Charlene. If you can, as we used to say in radio, "stay tuned," you'll get to know her and her story a bit better later when she shares a gem of a chapter called "7 Seeds of Service of the Peanut Butter Promise." It will include a lot of her testimony (bring Kleenex), and show how one person, her grandmother, set an example for her that was life changing. Its ripples of hope found Charlene—a hope she now passes on to any and all who'll receive it.

What I'm trying to show and share is that you can mess up as Charlene and I have and still be blessed to live long enough to enjoy a wonderful life. We wake up in deep gratitude every day, pinching ourselves that we are living nearly a picture-perfect life by way of the Peanut Butter Promise. We get that, maybe at this time, you may not think a comeback for you is possible. I don't want to talk smart, but do you think your story is any worse than mine or that of others? Be assured, friend, that you have not cornered the "mess up market." Been there, done that.

As a matter of fact, we're looking for a few imperfect people who may be able to relate to us and join us for an exciting, invigorating, and somewhat unpredictable journey on the path of the Peanut Butter Promise. If that's you, it does come with a responsibility, which is to understand that you *do* have a meaningful and unique purpose and you have an obligation to identify it and fulfill it. If that's you, great, but the calling on your mission also acknowledges that your clock is ticking, and that *now* will never come back, so the time for action is yesterday. OK, that's a stretch, but you get what I mean.

So what do you think? Do you want to join us? If so, we're here to help you every step of the way. We mean it; we're not just saying that.

That's a Peanut Butter Promise.

# CHAPTER 2

# 7 POWERS OF THE PEANUT BUTTER PROMISE

**P**riorities—we all have them. They are things we say are important to us; it's just a matter of if they are in the right order or not. Sometimes a story helps shed light on a topic.

In September of 1996, a few weeks after the release of my first book, *Leap of Faith: God Must Be a Packer Fan*, I was sitting with my friend Robert Brooks in his home. At the time, he was a tremendously popular star receiver for the Green Bay Packers football team. For those of you who may not be Packers fans (and I have no clue why you wouldn't be), the Lambeau Leap is a touchdown celebration performed after a touchdown by a Packers player at Lambeau Field. After exchanging high fives with teammates, the player bolts toward the stands in the back of the end zone and then leaps into the waiting arms of endearing fans.

Robert, who'd written the foreword for the book, was also on the front cover doing a Lambeau Leap. He began our conversation with, "Steve, congratulations on the book. It's great, man. People are talking about it; they're coming up to me asking me to autograph their book—even some on the Packers Cruise last week."

I asked him, "Robert, when did it occur to you that Packers fans are pretty crazy but very unique and special?"

Without missing a beat, he told me, "It was last year. I was open in the end zone when Brett Favre threw me a pass that was going about 217 miles an hour. I caught it for a touchdown. My hands were hurtin' so bad that instead of going to the sidelines and getting a few high fives that I knew would hurt, I decided to turn around and head to the back of the end zone and jump into the stands. So that's what I did. I jumped into the front row, and the next thing I know, I'm lying in the lap of this very pretty blonde-haired lady, who looked like she was about seventy. Steve, she's got a Cheese Head hat on her head and a big smile on her face, and she smells like a perfume factory. So there she is, looking up at me, and I have fans dumping popcorn on my back and beer into the earhole of my helmet."

He continued, "Steve, the more I looked at her, the more I realized that she kind of looked like June Cleaver with a Cheese Head hat on." (June was the mom on the '50s and '60s television show *Leave It to Beaver*.) That was quite a picture Robert had painted in my head! Then, he shared that he noticed one empty seat to the lady's left. This is significant because it is a well-known fact there are a lot of fans on the Packers' season ticket waiting list.

"Ma'am, whose empty seat is that?" he pointed.

"That's my husband's seat!"

"Where is he?" asked Brooks.

Still smiling, she yelled back, "He died!"

At that moment, Robert felt a bit foolish. He gave his condolences to the woman, but then he noticed something he had not seen seconds prior; he saw not one, but *two* empty seats to her right side! Robert couldn't resist trying to evoke an explanation for that, so he asked her one more question.

"Lady, whose seats are those?"

"My kids!" she said.

"Well, where are they?" Robert shouted.

Still smiling, she yelled, "They're at the funeral!"

Now, this story is not true, but if it were, it would provide us with a great parable of out-of-whack priorities. As we indicated at the top of this chapter, your priorities (and having them in the right order) is imperative for the fulfillment of your Peanut Butter Promise.

The seven powers of the Peanut Butter Promise contain edifying personal potentialities and, when accepted and effectively implemented, are able to catalyze the process of taking you on your journey to fulfill your purpose. Each and every one of these powers will play an important part for your success. Different ones will stand out to different people, depending on their life and their situation.

The seven powers of the Peanut Butter Promise are: **Purpose**, **Passion**, **Plan and Action**, **Perseverance**, **Personal Development**, **Positive Attitude**, and **Priorities**.

Here we go.

## 1. The Power of Purpose

In the subtitle of his *New York Times* bestseller *The Purpose Driven Life*, Rick Warren asked this great question: "What on Earth am I here for?" When we figure that out, what that calling is, we're on the verge of a breakthrough. I'm grateful that, from an early age, I had a calling on my life to help others. My purpose was to fulfill God's plan for my life.

If you know what your calling is and are operating in the joy of it on your journey to fulfilling your purpose, that's great. However, if you are not quite sure yet what your calling is, "Let not your heart be troubled," (John 14:1); the Peanut Butter Promise can help you!

In case you do not know what your calling is, here are seven questions that may help you.

1. As a child, what did you spend time daydreaming about doing?
2. What did you spend time pretending to do, or was there a person you wanted to be like?
3. What do others say you're good at doing?
4. If you were given $77,000,000, what would you do with it?
5. If you found out you had only seven months to live, what would you do?
6. What do you want your obituary to say about you?
7. If you had a guarantee that one goal would come true for you, what would it be?

Hopefully, these questions have given you some ideas. To be clear, we believe that true joy and success is only found or realized where and when we are operating in the gifts and talents of our purpose. I've certainly found this to be true, but it took me a lot longer to find the "sweet spot" of my God-given purpose.

Question one is significant. The answer to that could very well be a preview of a coming attraction for you. It will not happen for you right away, but if that vision is a part of your purpose, it's not a matter of *if*, but *when* it will happen.

For me, I practiced speaking and pretended to be on the radio in my room for hours, and so did others I met in the business. Pay attention to that, and if you're a parent, may I suggest you listen to your kids and what they want to do as well. As a bonus, more than learning what they want to do, you may learn more about who they are. If you can help them identify their purpose, that will be a good thing, not only for them, but for everyone.

Question number two asked differently would be, "What person would you like to switch places with for a day or two?" Once you have identified the person or persons, acknowledge them, and then celebrate that you need not become them. You're fine being you and knowing that you're good enough—that you have been engineered and designed for something great, something so special, even the person you'd change places with cannot do it.

Question number three suggests that if you are not sure what your unique talents and abilities are, ask a few of your peers. I think you'll be pleased to hear their enthusiasm on the subject of you, and they might share an idea or two about a gift you may possess that you may never have considered or paid attention to.

Question number four: What would you do if you were to receive $77 million dollars? This is meant to spur you to thinking about what you would do if you had no worries about cash. Maybe you'll never have $77 million, but faithfully working from the Peanut Butter Promise can inspire, and possibly help you, give a few hundred to The Salvation Army or another cause of your choice, and that would feel pretty good, wouldn't it?

Questions five through seven deal with urgency, if you learned you had only a short time to live. Maybe instead of dealing with whether you had seven months to live, how about answering what you would do if you only had seven hours to live. If this were the case, who would you reach out to? Are a few of those people ones that you should be reaching out to now?

What you would want your obituary to say about what you have accomplished pretty much sums up what you should be doing sooner rather than later. Lastly, what would you dare to dream if you were given a guarantee that it *would* come true? The last question is quite revealing, and we must pay very close attention to the answer. It is there that we could very well find the jackpot to purpose, passion, peace, and all the other benefits to be possessed on the journey to fulfilling your purpose.

The great Earl Nightingale, one of the pioneers in the personal development field, said this: "Not achieving your purpose is like a piece of dynamite not exploding." We couldn't agree more, and that's why we are here to help you fulfill your purpose and go out with a boom.

In Ken Blanchard's book, *The Heart of a Leader*, he makes this strong statement: "Purpose has to do with one's calling—the business you're in as a person." When we know our calling, we have a sense of urgency, and that is always good because some of us have learned that life goes fast. The obituary column is a constant reminder that tomorrow is not promised to us. Heck, our next hour—our next breath—is not promised to us. With this in mind, the time for action is now!

Leading authority on the subject, Kevin McCarthy, speaker and author of *The On-Purpose Person*, reminds us that, "Our identity is who we are, and that is a child of God. Our activity is what we do—

our job, or area of service." They're quite different and need to be separated. That is a powerful point and one that the Peanut Butter Promise submits to you and asks you to deeply ponder.

## 2. The Power of Passion

Nothing quite releases the power of passion in a person than when, as just discussed, they are living on-purpose—that is, operating within your talents, abilities, and gifts of your life's calling—that is, doing what you're supposed to be doing. If you are doing what you want, or are supposed to be doing, great. If not, keep reading; the Peanut Butter Promise can help.

What activity or work makes you feel good about who you are while you are doing it? Chances are that's what is, or could become, your passion, giving you a joy for living. Have you ever watched people do what they love to do? They are energetic souls; in 77.7 percent of these cases (percentage is mine), these people have found their passion and are on the fast track to fulfilling their Peanut Butter Promise.

People of passion are loaded with enthusiasm; they "love the game," and they're always trying to get better, especially in their area of expertise. They realize if they are not getting better, they are falling behind. They're constantly learning; they have a bounce in their step, a smile on their face and also in their voice. A couple examples of passion-in-action people that I've seen are Wayne Larrivee, Kevin Harlan, and Mark Peterson. Wayne is the radio play-by-play voice of the Green Bay Packers, and his enthusiastic observations make you feel like you are at the game.

When I asked Wayne where his passion comes from, he said, "My passion for work is rooted in my love of the games. It is a thrill to be at the game and accurately documenting it!"

I also see and hear deep passion in the voice of our friend Kevin Harlan, who you can hear as an announcer for the NFL on CBS and NBA on TNT.

Mark has been a physical education teacher for thirty-three years. Mark dives passionately headfirst into everything he does. He writes a column called "Coach P's Corner" for the local paper, and if you read it, his optimism shows. Mark says, "My passion really comes from working with other people. I love working with kids and teaching them. I love coaching, it gives me a chance to teach other things besides sports."

What are your passions? What are the things you love to do? What are the activities that give you such joy that while you are engaged in them, you lose all track of time? What is it that you would do for no pay, and when you stand back from that activity, you feel satisfied? Before we move on, this hope-and-encouragement-filled philosophy gives this caution: Make sure you are pouring your passions into the right things. That's something true Peanut Butter Promise Players are always doing, and they do it passionately.

## 3. The Power of Plan and Action

Do you suppose that a corporate CEO gets together with his presidents, vice presidents, and sales people on the first of the year and says something like this: "Well, team, it's another year. We have a great company, you are great people, let's just go out and do the best we can do!" Of course, not. Rather, CEOs share business plans that amass many pages, including budgets of sales and expenses they monitor very closely. I've known great accountants who can make Abraham Lincoln scream. I mean, they watch every penny, and as individuals, we should be and do no different.

We'll bring you the help in this area in chapter six, "The DreamGoal Achievement Program." When a builder is asked to build a house, does he just get some wood and nails and start building? Nope, he sits down with the ones who will be living in and, more importantly, paying for the house. He drafts a blueprint and follows it to completion. This takes out all the guesswork and saves a lot of time.

If we are looking to drive on a seven-hundred-mile trip to an unknown destination, what do we do? We get a road map or, to bring this up to date, we would get a GPS. This is necessary because we know that one innocent-but-wrong turn can cost us time and money. The thing about getting lost on the road of life, or in a car on the highway, is that we're never sure when we got lost.

Years ago, my brother Dale and I were returning home from a two-day Peanut Butter Promise event. I was driving. It was a beautiful summer day as we breezed along with the windows down. We came to a town called Juneau. The name of the high school was Dodgeland, which was noted in bold letters on the side of the building. As we chatted, I proceeded up a hill and through town until we were safely out of town.

Strangely, about twenty minutes later, we entered a town and looking to our right, we were shocked to see the side of a school that read: "Dodgeland High School!" This left us both perplexed with the same question: How did we end up going through Juneau again? To this very day, Dale and I have no clue how that happened, but we clearly took a wrong turn somewhere.

One of the most honest and bold souls on any subject of human realities is author and pastor Andy Stanley. He sums up the need for a map in his book, *The Principle of the Path*. In this work, he makes this statement: "Direction—not intention—determines destination." Translation: It matters not where we *assume* we are or where we are headed, but where we are *really* going. The good news is if we don't like the direction we are going, we can change it in an instant, but it's important to determine sooner, rather than later, that we are lost.

Accurate Plans and Actions are crucial time-savers; they can put and keep you on the right road and save you from having to go through Juneau twice.

## 4. The Power of Perseverance

Neither ants nor streams stop for anything, and perseverance is like that. Perseverance, which is committing to finish and accomplish something, is crucial to achieving our worthy DreamGoals or fulfilling our purpose. Just as much a part of the process is patience, which, upon reflection, is a form of faith-in-action choosing not to complain during the journey, and choosing *not* to quit, regardless of the situation.

To persevere is to continue to make your way up from what feels like the bottom of the ocean, fighting the pressure of the water and waves on the way to the surface. I've known many people who not only hit, but crashed at the bottom, and would not have been faulted for giving up or quitting but got help and plowed forward, receiving a reward beyond what they could ever think or imagine.

One such person is our friend Chester Marcol, who appears with us at Peanut Butter Promise events. He was the 1972 NFL Rookie of the Year as a placekicker for the Green Bay Packers. Everything was going along fantastically well until someone introduced him to cocaine in 1980. Not good. That addiction and other poor choices took him down a path of total destruction. Head Coach Bart Starr had to fire Chester, who more than lost his job he was also in a struggle to not lose his mind.

Years later, after dozens of half-hearted attempts in rehab, many just to dry out and rest, Chester decided he was going to commit suicide. He mixed a concoction of rat poison, battery acid, and vodka. He quickly chugged the contents and did what any irrational person would do in that moment: He ran to the bedroom to lie down and die; that was the plan. The next thing he knew, he was throwing up. He then watched as the vomit burned the carpet as if a match had lit it!

Chester shares about his arduous comeback during our webinars, PBP rallies, and other events. It's a long story that can be read in his incredible book with Gary D'Amato called *Alive and Kicking: My Journey Through Football, Addiction and Life*. Today, Chester is a highly successful professional addictions counselor who has deep compassion for those afflicted. One of his lines that I like is "I'm glad life isn't fair because if it was, I'd be dead." Wow. To those of us like my wife and me who came out of addictions, that is a sobering comment. (If you go to our site at PeanutButterPromise.com or search YouTube, you should find a two-part podcast we did with Chester.)

People of perseverance have a postage stamp philosophy in that they stick faithfully to their assignment until it gets to where it's supposed to go. They have the "ant philosophy." Have you ever watched ants? They are fast-moving, they know where they are going, and are on a mission to do their work. Have you ever put your foot in front of one? What do they do? They walk over it, around it; they keep going until they get past the obstacle. We need to take a good lesson from that.

Perseverance has been a much-needed quality for Charlene and me. We're not the most talented people in the world. There are certainly people more qualified to be writing this book, but we decided we would take the hundreds of hours to invest our past pain and suffering in this work to help others. Like many of you, we've spent a good share of time in the desert, feeling discouraged and wanting to quit. But because we did not, you're reading this. Today, we have peace and joy unspeakable. The blessings we've seen are exceedingly above and beyond what we could ever think or imagine.

Friend, what we are trying to say is at those moments when you want to "hang it up," don't! It is then when it is most important to choose an expectant and positive attitude and keep moving forward. If you do, you'll get to where you feel led to be going, and we hope that is to fulfill your God-given purpose with the help of the Peanut Butter Promise.

## 5. The Power of a Positive Attitude

Many an expert in the field of personal growth and human potential feel that choosing to live with positive attitude is as important to peace, prosperity, and fulfilling our purpose as anything. Straight from a little league diamond is this lesson from Thor, a player for the Cougars, to show and share what a positive attitude looks and sounds like.

Before many of the kids' parents got to their seats, the visiting Lions had bitten first, launching a torrid hitting tirade. So much so that the home team Cougars found themselves trailing after the top of the first inning by a score of 17–0! After the seemingly endless quest to get the Lions to make the third out, some of the nine-year-old players on the Cougars hung their heads, some even sobbing, as they made the journey back to their bench. But Thor, to the amusement of the crowd, came sprinting in from right field.

Upon arriving at the bench, while many of his teammates sulked, he grabbed his helmet and bat, took a few practice cuts, and proceeded to enthusiastically make his way to home plate. It was then that his manager, Mr. Kane, perplexed by the young man's enthusiasm, reached out and grabbed Thor by the elbow.

He looked into his eyes and asked him this question: "Thor, why in the dickens are you so pumped? Didn't you see what happened to us out there? For crying out loud, the Lions just scored seventeen runs against us!"

Without missing a beat, Thor, with big eyes gleaming, looked up and reminded him of one very important fact. "Yeah, Coach, I know, but we haven't been up to bat yet!"

Something Thor certainly understood was that the game had just begun, that his team still had plenty of at-bats/chances to win the game. It's certainly during these times in our lives that we sometimes could use an attitude adjustment.

The legendary Earl Nightingale, in his astounding audio series, *Lead the Field*, said, "Our attitudes deal with our feelings, moods, and actions." The Peanut Butter Promise recognizes that, every day, we are presented with hundreds of opportunities to make a choice to remain optimistic. We hope for the best for others and ourselves, taking constant confident action to persevere through all things, even when the going is rough—and there will always be rough-going.

Our friend Brian Tracy says a positive attitude is the appropriate response to stress. Zig Ziglar was asked the question: What will positive thinking let you do?

Answer: Positive thinking will let you use your ability and experience to the maximum. That is realistic. To believe positive thinking will let you do anything is tantamount to disaster. It's untrue and very damaging because it creates false hope and unrealistic expectations, and those are the seedbed for depression. A few pages later, he said, "No, a positive attitude won't let you do anything, but it will let you do everything better than negative thinking will."

Although keeping a positive attitude is a great choice, it requires always being realistic. From the world of "a positive attitude will only take you so far" comes this personal story. I was in the YMCA parking lot heading to my car. Because my mind and memory were not quite what they used to be, I made it a point to park in relatively the same place, on the second level, depending on availability, of course. I headed to my car, where I proceeded to put my key in the door, turned it, but it would not open the lock. I pulled it out and tried it again. Still, it would not budge. I yanked it out and looked at it to make sure it was my car key. It was. After a few more fruitless attempts, I stood up, somewhat exhausted, stunned, perplexed, and every other word that describes confusion and frustration.

Two seconds later, I gazed over the top of this car to the one next to it, and the mystery was solved. I walked over to the car that was two spots down from this car, put the key in the door, and voilà, it unlocked with ease. It was then I realized I had been trying to unlock a door to a car that was not mine, but it was an exact make and model as mine!

Right after the episode, one of the first things that crossed my mind was the embarrassment I would have experienced if the owner of the car I was trying to open had walked over, catching me trying to steal their car! So I quickly motored out and spent the entire journey home reflecting on the experience. My goodness, I thought I had the right key. I thought it would open the door right away. Why, one of the times I cranked on the key, I even prayed, while keeping a positive attitude, that the door would open. But, of course, it wouldn't, and we know why: Because I was trying to unlock a door with a key to the wrong car.

Like me, do you have keys and are trying to open the wrong doors, despite having a positive attitude? A positive attitude and thinking is great, but it would behoove us to make sure we're pushing in and cranking with the right key into the right door, lest the door to our DreamGoals that lead to fulfilling our purpose may never open.

We watch the *Dr. Phil* show whenever we can, and on the subject of a positive attitude, he says, "There is good news and bad news. The bad news is the only person you can control is yourself. The good news is that the only person you need to control is yourself." I believe this goes along with being able to choose and control our attitude—in this case, to choose a positive one. I saw an acronym one time that said ACE. The A was for attitude; the C was for concentration; the E for effort, and upon deeper reflection, those are really the only three things as human beings we can control.

Peanut Butter Promise Players know that attitudes are contagious. They look in the mirror and ask this good question: "Is mine worth catching?" They invest ample amounts of time in a good personal development program, and they realize the bigger the tree, the more its roots must be planted securely to withstand storms. They understand that the taller the building, the deeper the foundation must be. They know the only chance they have to fulfill their purpose is to dig and take the gold from their own mine, and a good personal development program is the only chance to capitalize and profit on the treasures that lie within them and the others they serve.

## 6. The Power of Personal Development

What's personal development? It involves making a commitment to become the best person we can become by using our God-given talents, abilities, and gifts. Many times, it requires a change in our thinking, actions, and behaviors. It requires a disciplined plan and action based on the gathered knowledge used wisely to develop good habits that propel us toward our purpose and destiny. Engaging in a consistent personal development program can move one rapidly from no-mentum to momentum, and more swiftly than one could ever imagine.

A key word here is "change." When I hit the bottom and entered treatment for alcoholism, I needed to change, badly. If I had chosen to sit in my recovery group or pay no mind to my counselors, then when I got out, there's a good chance I may have gone back to the same practices and behaviors. I've long believed that bad behavior cannot be incarcerated. What I mean is there are people who go to prison for crimes, and rightfully so, but my wife and I have come to believe that rehabilitation is the key to change.

Charlene and I had a wonderful path we used to walk near our place on a beautiful lake. Nothing was more peaceful than being out on a nice, sunny day. There was a portion of the journey that was treacherous and that was when we would go past a residence where there were two vicious dogs. I'm not sure why, but "Mutt" and "Jeff" didn't seem to like us. When they saw us, thank goodness, their owner pulled on their leashes to save us from annihilation. There was no question that if those beasts had their way, we would have lost our faces.

Let's just say that happened. The local police would have showed up, and with the owners saying, "Bad doggies," they would have then led the dogs away to "Doggie Prison," where they would spend one year in captivity (which is like seven in dog years). Let's say that while they were locked up in their kennels, they did not receive any therapy or training to change their thinking or modify their behavior. Once they were released back to their owners, the question we pose is "What would those dogs do when Charlene and I came walking past them?" Our guess is that because they were still the same dogs, just like before, they probably would have sought to attack us and tear our faces off, right?

This dog scenario shows that more than wet babies are in need of change. We do too, in our thinking and behaviors, if we are truly serious about fulfilling our purpose. We need a good, consistent, and sound personal development program to accomplish that. My journey into this exciting area began on that day in 1977 when my father took me to that PMA rally where I heard Zig Ziglar and the others. I was not engaged in this practice until June 23, 1994. This was after the radio station had been sold and I had a lot of extra time. The bulk of my program involved listening to audio tapes in my car. I'd just received some new cassette albums from a motivational speaker I had never heard of named Jim Rohn.

Without a cassette player in my car, I had to improvise, so I loaded tapes into a small boom box that I placed on the dash of my car, just below the rearview mirror, which worked well most of the time. The adventure came when I was in town and took a corner a little too fast, and the player would slide across the dash. I'd watch helplessly and listen as the player would smash on the floor mat, spewing the four batteries it contained.

Those were unforgettable and valuable times, listening to Jim Rohn's six-tape series called *The Art of Exceptional Living*. It was just the right one for me, at just the right time. One of many of the profound thoughts and ideas he shared was taking time to read and listen to tapes about your chosen field. I can assure you this has been part of my miracle, and I'd suggest it for you as well. Jim made many revelatory statements in his life, but one I grasped in his book, *The Treasury of Quotes*, points out that every home worth $250,000 has a library. I get the point. He said, "Leaders are readers."

May I suggest that, as part of a personal development program, you set aside at least a half hour a day to read something inspirational or something in your field of expertise? As part of our program, Charlene and I view inspiring television every day, including Joyce Meyer, Joel Osteen, TD Jakes, Pastor Charles Stanley, and his son, Pastor Andy Stanley. We read scripture and the devotional *My Utmost for His Highest* by Oswald Chambers. We also do the best we can without going overboard to enjoy a well-balanced diet, get exercise four to five times per week, and try to get plenty of sleep. That's what we do; the key is to find out what works best for you. Don't go too far overboard or be too critical of yourself. Remember, the Peanut Butter Promise is a progress-not-perfection program.

I wouldn't be giving this power credence if I didn't mention that my father was the greatest mentor for me in this area. His personal library held thousands of books, many classics I absorbed as part of the research for this book. Dad always wanted to learn more. He was a voracious reader, and I am grateful I caught that bug, as well as the many other great things he taught me. As a matter of fact, you can see the library if you tune into *The Peanut Butter Promise Power-Encouragement* Podcast. You can find links at PeanutButterPromise. com, or feel free to subscribe to our YouTube channel, become a friend on Facebook, or follow us on Twitter.

Personal development in unison with good self-discipline is positively life changing; it takes people in the middle of the pack to the lead. They not only learn from their own experiences, but those of others. Many of the world's personal development and potential leaders profess that those that implement an effective program that includes keeping a "To-Do" list, learning valuable lessons from mistakes, and establishing good habits are the ones on their way to fulfilling their Peanut Butter Promise, and we couldn't agree more.

## 7. The Power of Priorities

Have you ever been told your priorities are out of order? *The Oxford English Dictionary* says a priority is "a thing that is regarded as more important than another." They can be matters we say are important to us, but the fact of the matter is our true priorities are revealed through our actions. During one of my recovery group meetings someone made this remark: "Who you are speaks so loudly I can't hear what you're saying." Ouch—for that, I am guilty. In those groups, I was also reminded that actions do speak louder than words. People would rather see a sermon than hear one any day.

This is an area that certainly provides an element of tension, but it's a subject we all must deal with. Properly aligned priorities are absolutely imperative, and doing things right (with the utmost of integrity) is imperative to succeeding. I now want to share another story about priorities, but unlike the pathetic tale I dropped on you earlier about the Packer womaniac, this one is true.

Ginny Boyke heard the phone ring and proceeded to promptly answer it.

"Hello, this is the Boykes."

She listened closely as the caller tersely identified himself, told her why he was calling, and on whose behalf. He didn't let her get a word in edgewise. She simply nodded as he made his pitch. It took the farmer's wife only a few seconds to determine this was no ordinary call, and the request being made on the other end was quite extraordinary and came with an invitation for a once-in-a-lifetime opportunity, so she handed the phone to her husband.

"Hi, this is Clarence."

The stoic and quite business-like voice on the other end identified himself and his role and quickly reviewed with the patriarch of the home what he'd just shared with his wife. As he listened for a minute, Clarence was impressed but not swayed.

"Uh, sir, that is a gracious invitation," he informed the man, "but we already have a commitment for Saturday, April third."

Now, I would have loved to have had my nosy ears on that line, just as some used to when families (like mine) had party lines and could listen in on others' calls back in the '60s. Anyway, I have more than a hunch that upon hearing Clarence's uncompromising and unwavering answer, the fellow on the other end of the long-distance call was shocked, actually *really* shocked by what Clarence told him. You see, the man on the other end of the line was representing a pretty, no *very* important guy who represented a pretty important office. Let me further explain before we share, as Paul Harvey would say, *The Rest of the Story*.

It just so happened that date discussed with Clarence and Virginia Boyke clashed with the upcoming wedding of their son Gary. It was for that reason they would not, for even a second, have considered accepting the invitation from Gerald Ford—yes, Gerald Ford—who, at that time, was the president of the United States of America! His office was phoning to ask if they could visit Boyke's farm that Saturday morning and have breakfast with them, and they were turned down!

I mean, really, who turns down the president of the United States? This was an opportunity that would have provided them with fond memories of family and farm photo opportunities that would have lasted a lifetime. But Clarence and Ginny had their priorities in order, and on Saturday, April 3, 1976, with no regret whatsoever, the proud parents dressed to the nines as their son Gary became one with his wife, Rose, and they are still going strong today.

The Boykes have always been very humble people. As a matter of fact, my parents, who were longtime best friends of the family, did not know this story. Clarence died in 1997 and Ginny in 2000. They certainly had their priorities in order. How about us? We should regularly ask ourselves, *Am I valuing my family over my work, or am I valuing projects over people?*

Personal growth and potential authorities, such as Zig Ziglar, Brian Tracy, and Hal Urban, agree that finding true peace and true success are wrapped up in keeping personal priorities in their proper order, and to that, there is no argument from the Peanut Butter Promise.

# CHAPTER 3

# 7 PRINCIPLES OF THE PEANUT BUTTER PROMISE

I'm not crazy about going to the dentist, especially when I need to have a tooth removed. When I was a kid, I went to a dentist who apparently had only half of a degree from dental school. What happened was, as he was twisting and cranking on my tooth, it broke in half! So years later, I was very hesitant to have our dentist, Dr. Ruth Canal, yank one of mine. However, because of the pain I was experiencing, I relented. I did ask her to take a pledge before she began.

"Doctor, would you please raise your hand and promise me that you will pull the tooth, the whole tooth, and nothing but the tooth, so help you God?" OK, that was maybe a tacky way to bring the word truth into this conversation, but it seemed like the right place to insert that joke. But there is nothing to joke about where honesty and integrity are involved, which we will be broaching shortly. It is an area that Peanut Butter Promise Players need to reckon and reconcile with in the moment-by-moment battery of choices we make.

The seven principles of the Peanut Butter Promise contain character traits, disciplines, and skills when studied, and when applied reveal untapped talents, abilities, and gifts in us that provide the impetus to bring about positive results to launch us toward fulfilling our purpose.

This portion of the work makes the case that, at the earliest time possible in our life, we should seek and find our purpose and then set a plan into motion to fulfill our purpose.

The seven principles of the Peanut Butter Promise are: **Integrity, Responsibility, Self-Discipline, Excellence, Cooperation, Communication**, and **Association**.

Let's get started.

## 1. The Principle of Integrity

Integrity is a good word, a strong word, one that is at the very heart of fulfilling our purpose. Integrity is much broader than just being honest with ourselves and others; it encapsulates and encompasses so much of our lives. A local restaurant where Charlene and I enjoy a nice meal has a self-service beverage area. I usually order water with meals. With an ice-filled cup in hand, I find the H2O, noticing that it is right next to the lemonade. It is then when an unruly voice in my head whispers, *You know, Steve, it's hot out; no one would know if you added a bit of lemonade to your water just to add a little taste to it. I mean, really, nobody would know you didn't pay for the lemonade. Why not grab a little?*

I'm pleased to share that I've never really considered doing that, but I'm not above temptation—I've had my victories and losses—and believe me, I'm working hard at more victories.

All solid, trusting relationships, such as marriages, family, friends, and work relationships, must be built on a rock of integrity for them to be sustained and last. I like this from the 1969 book from Earl Nightingale called *This is Earl Nightingale,* where he said, "Integrity is the quality we most often look for in others. It is what a woman wants in her husband, and he in her. It is what the boss wants of his employees, and vice versa. Integrity is the world's most valuable quality in a service, product or a person."

I've learned that a good night's sleep can only be experienced while sleeping on a pillow of integrity. Integrity is built through trust, which takes time, and it can be lost in seconds. One day, I noticed a leak coming from a pipe below the sink. I set a pail under it, and a few hours later, there wasn't much water in it, but when I checked it the next day, I was surprised by how much there was. To make matters worse, I accidently knocked the pail over! Our integrity is a bit like that in that it can take a long time to fill the bucket drip by drip, but with one kick (mistake), we can lose it all.

Integrity doesn't come with levels; you either have it, or you don't. It can take years to build, and can be lost quickly through one poor choice, but many times, integrity is lost not by a blowout but, rather, a slow leak.

Here is a question I like to ask in situations where integrity is involved: *Is what I'm doing or saying trust-building or trust-burning?* It has made me stop before proceeding with a comment or activity. At the heart of that question is this: *Is what I am doing or saying of the utmost integrity?* That is a question that has served me well.

Integrity can only be developed as we build our character, and one of the world's leaders in the world of potential, Dr. John Maxwell, says this: "If you want to build your character, you need to align four things: your values, your thinking, your feelings, and your actions." Boy, do I need work on those, along with remembering that the Peanut Butter Promise is a progress-not-perfection program. I'm constantly reminded that I am a "work in progress," and that's OK because as long as I live in integrity, there is hope for me.

## 2. The Principle of Responsibility

Taking 100 percent personal responsibility for our life can be difficult, but it is a critical factor and step to maturity, getting us on, and helping us remain on the path of the Peanut Butter Promise. After getting into treatment for alcoholism in 1991, I wondered how all of this could have happened to such a wonderful guy like me. I must confess I spent a lot of time (that was wasted) looking for some people to blame. Then, I remembered my buddy Brad Vivoda, who was such a help in the early days of my recovery.

One day, he said, "Steve, someday, I'm going to make a 'Problem Finder.'"

"Oh, that sounds cool. What will that be?" I probed.

He said, "It will be a chain around the neck that has a mirror attached to it. When you have a problem, just look in the mirror, and most of the time, you'll find the problem."

I'm not sure if Brad ever got that one produced and submitted for a patent, but if not, he should. So, I sat in my recovery group, being challenged to look in the mirror, and when I did, I found the problem; it was me!

The word "responsibility" broken down is "response ability," meaning we have the ability to respond appropriately in all situations. Of course, this isn't necessarily easy. It may take lots of time and practice, but it can be done.

Here are three suggestions to help with taking responsibility as it relates to the Peanut Butter Promise. They are:

**Get out of denial.** What we're getting at here is learning to deal with reality in all things and situations. What that looked like for me was getting out of denial and admitting to God, *I am an alcoholic whose priorities are way out of whack. I am behind on my bills and my dreams and desperately need help*. Until I took that step, there was no hope for me. This principle doesn't discriminate. We all have to get real and deal with our stuff because if we don't, it will continue to deal with us.

**Stop blaming others.** If you're angry with someone for what he/she has done to you, it must be dealt with. I believe the greatest counselor of our time is Dr. Phil McGraw, who says the following about taking responsibility:

"You are one hundred percent *not* responsible for what happened to you in the past. But you *are* one hundred percent responsible for what you do about it." Is it time to stop blaming others, get help, and move on to give you the best chance to fulfill your Peanut Butter Promise? Reviewing number one may help, but you may also want to reread the line where Dr. Phil urges us to not blame others for where we are, and if you can't handle that, don't blame me, but him.

**Forgive others and yourself.** We've all had people we have wronged and those who have wronged us. One thing Dad burned into me was to not let things people are saying or doing bother you, that life is too short and time is too precious to harbor any bad feelings toward others. It's easier said than done, but it's a universal law that as long as we hold anything against others, we will not have peace. The other person that maybe needs to be forgiven is you. When we do this, we prove we are serious by choosing to take action immediately and move forward with a clear sense of purpose and positive attitude.

## 3. The Principle of Self-Discipline

My pal, Robert Brooks, who, for a time, was the premier "Lambeau Leaper of the Packers," was probably one of the finest physical specimens I've ever been around. He was chiseled, 177 pounds, and lean. Kent Johnson, the team's strength and condition coordinator, told me once that Robert was always at 177 pounds on weigh day, and at six feet tall, that was pretty good.

And there was a reason he looked and felt so good. It was because of his incredible self-discipline in many areas, but in this case what he was putting into his body was where he was doing something different from me. For one, he was drinking two concoctions everyday that could kill a raccoon. Me, I was eating two delicious Concrete Mixers from Culver's restaurant every week. On many occasions, I'd observe Robert in his kitchen, where he put food (he called it nutrition) into a blender that, to me, only seemed fit for our childhood dog, Buster, who used to eat stones—no, really, he did. Robert would hit a button on his machine, and soon, he'd be pouring the contents into not one, but two, glasses. What I suspected he was doing happened when he set one glass before me.

"Here, Steve, try some of this."

He chugged his, and I took more than a swig of mine.

"Oh, God, Robert that stuff is awful! How can you drink that?"

He laughed at me as I did everything I could to not projectile vomit on the marble countertop.

A couple of other former 1996 Super Bowl champion Packers who were extremely disciplined were Don Beebe and my friend Adam Timmerman. The truth is where you find champions and worthy accomplishment, you will find tons of self-discipline. To reach our goals, we must pay full price—and in advance.

Peanut Butter Promise Players love self-discipline; they have established and kept good boundaries in all areas of their life. It may not always have been that way, but anyone who has attempted or is attempting to accomplish anything worthy, including fulfilling their purpose, totally understands that assertion. As a matter of fact, the Peanut Butter Promise, like many of the other highly effective personal growth potential philosophies, is adamant that *nothing* good, and that means *nothing truly* good, comes into or leaves our life, devoid of the practice of personal self-discipline.

There is so much that can be placed under this umbrella. Being self-disciplined involves taking charge of our life (accepting 100 percent responsibility for our future), bringing our thoughts, emotions, and subsequent actions and behaviors under control. Any of the prominent personal potential authorities will profess that this is a key step in becoming the person you were meant to become. A huge enemy of self-discipline could very well be self-deception. It's easy to deceive ourselves by thinking we can put off doing certain non-pleasant assignments.

In his Nightingale-Conant book, *Insights Into Achievement*, Brian Tracy says the following on the subject of self-discipline: "It is a combination of conscious actions, but also the realization of the consequences of certain actions and inactions." As indicated, for me, that translates to what I put in my mouth, or when I choose (usually through a lame excuse) to not have a solid "To-Do" list and choosing instead to fill time with an activity that brings more gratification to the present moment than what I should be doing.

In his bestselling Nightingale-Conant audio tape cassette series, *The Psychology of Winning,* Dr. Denis Waitley asks, "Is what you are doing goal-achieving or tension-relieving?" Ouch. That one hits way too close to home for me. Self-discipline many times starts with developing healthy habits and learning the practice of self-control in all circumstances. *The Pocket Oxford Dictionary* defines a habit this way: something a person does regularly. We all have habits, both good ones and bad ones.

One of the best illustrations I have seen is how habits are a bit like cables. We are speaking of the thick and heavy ones made up of many, many thin wires that, when woven over the top of each other many times, become very strong, practically unbreakable. Good ones take us closer to our goal; on the other hand, our bad ones weigh us down. The topic of self-discipline and the development of good habits is very important. We suggest you seek other sources of information and counsel on the subject. The Bible has much to say on the topic; Brian Tracy and Jim Rohn are two people we have studied who have strong opinions and applications on the subject of self-discipline.

Experts agree that bad habits cannot be broken, but can be replaced with good ones, which we have found to be true, but much prayer and patience is involved in that program.

Take a look at the people around you who are truly successful, and we believe you will find they practice loads of positive self-discipline, have tight "To-Do" lists, and have learned that the biggest time-saving and belly fat-shrinking word is "no." And when confronted, they will actually tell you they have learned to love self-discipline—not the process, but its magnificent benefits that lurch them daily toward the fulfillment of their purpose.

It's always wise to deal with our bad habits sooner rather than later, not just by slashing away at the cobwebs, but killing the spider—that is, getting to the root of the problem and making proper adjustments.

I can tell you from experience (and I'm still learning) that self-control and discipline will be a lifelong challenge, but my program has provided me with many benefits, and it will for you too.

## 4. The Principle of Excellence

My father, who was my greatest inspiration here on Earth, used to remind me often, "If it's worth doing, it's worth doing right." What he was trying to teach me is the importance of doing things with excellence. I have not even scratched the surface to mastering the material of which you are reading; I say, "Do as I say, but don't watch me too close!" Learning to do things better will be an eternal challenge for me, but like you, I'm working on it.

One thing that is obvious is that true Peanut Butter Promise Players are excellent at what they do in their chosen field. I am a firm believer that we shouldn't spend loads of time trying to do things that can be best done by others. I'm a taker of the advice to delegate areas of work or tasks to others who are more proficient than you—when this is possible, of course.

For example, I am not real tech savvy, so that is why, when computer issues come up, it is best for me to refer them to Charlene. If she doesn't have a solution, we then take them to our right-hand man, Mike Utech. For thirty years, he has been solving problems in this area for me, and now us. We'll say, "Hey, Mike, we need a website." With manual in hand and the patience of Job, he'll figure it out.

I've had the joy of knowing and working with many people who are excellent at what they do. One example is former Green Bay Packers professional football team president Bob Harlan, who served as its president until 2007. He was the architect of bringing a Super Bowl trophy to "Titletown" in the 1996 season. Not only is he one of the nicest and most gracious people I have ever known, but he was one of the most excellent leaders I've ever known.

He's been such a wonderful example and mentor to me. During one of our meetings, I asked him what it was that made him so good, so excellent at what he did, and he said this: "Steve, first of all, I hired the right people." In his most successful venture, this was hiring Ron Wolf as the general manager. He then brought aboard a head coach by the name of Mike Holmgren. One of the first trades they made was to get a seldom-used and highly unknown young quarterback from the Atlanta Falcons. You may have heard of him. His name is Brett Favre. Two years later, in 1993, in came the minister of defense, Reggie White. And then, three years later came a Super Bowl championship.

So, the first thing excellent leaders do is hire good people. What is second? Bob told me this: "After you hire the right people, you tell them *what* you want them to do. And the third thing is to let them *do* it." Of course, he confessed that it wasn't always easy to watch, as he witnessed decisions that would not have been his own, but he had taken the responsibility to let them, win or lose, and in Bob's case, the Packers won more than they lost.

I've had the honor to meet and talk with a few people who were excellent at their craft and what they were passionate about. One person was Myron Floren, the accordion player from the Lawrence Welk orchestra. Wow, I saw him play once. He was unbelievable! Another duo is Ben Peterson and his older brother John Peterson. They were wrestling champions in 1972 at the Olympics in Munich and 1976 in Montreal. As "iron sharpens iron, another sharpens another." (Proverbs 27:17). John recently confirmed to me that they definitely made each other better at what they were doing and what they wanted to achieve, which was to become excellent wrestlers. John won a gold medal in '72 and a silver medal in '76, while Ben won a silver medal in '72 and a gold medal in 1976.

Peanut Butter Promise Players become excellent at what they do. They realize that if it doesn't pay well now, in a matter of time, they will become so valuable, they will be paid sufficiently—not for what they do, but how well they do it. That excellence at what they do will sustain them through inevitable storms, ones that could blow others off the path of excellence, but not Peanut Butter Promise Players who know that as they grind, they will get to where they are headed: the fulfillment of their purpose and destiny.

## 5. The Principle of Cooperation

If you're going to fulfill your purpose and limit frustrations, it is imperative to learn the skill of cooperation, which is the ability to work well with others. If you have come to the conclusion by now that we need each other, you'd be right; that's why Peanut Butter Promise Partners appear in our life at just the right time to help us.

Cooperation is being able to work together with our fellow man toward a common goal. This can be among family or friends, but the truest sense may be in the corporate arena, where it's required among hundreds of individuals, even thousands. To be clear, good cooperation requires much self-control, including managing our emotions, which, for me, is an eternal battle. That means we have to be able to respond well and take responsibility for our words and actions. There is that responsibility word again.

I'd like to share what I feel may very well be one of the greatest examples of cooperation. It involves my redeemed and now even-tempered brother Dale, who worked for over forty years at Mercury Racing, which is a division of Mercury Marine, the world leader in its field. His story is amazing for many reasons, not limited to the fact that for over twenty-five of them, he drove nearly a hundred miles round-trip to work. In our area, we get snow, and that requires caution and patience. I love my brothers; we come from different talent sets. He may be a little more like Mom, who is laid-back. I'm like Dad, always on the move and a leader. Neither of these facts makes either of us better or worse than the other.

Dale spent over forty years with that company, most of them in a cubicle. Although he did not begin to get paid until 7 a.m., it was his usual practice to arrive at the office at six, but to be fair, that was his choice to come in early. My point through revealing this is the corporate world can be brutal in that it can be demanding, and there can be unfair deadlines and bosses who can be equally as demanding.

Now, Dale had great bosses, but it goes without saying that some of them had bad days and that spills over, and employees have to be able to take it, and for forty years, he did. And I'm telling you, there is no way I could have had that level of cooperation, but Dale did because that type of work and his type of cooperation allowed him to persevere, and he retired with honor and great accolades and commentary from his coworkers and superiors.

In retrospect, the best people I have worked for, who have been most cooperative, are very patient souls, ones who are able to keep their emotions in check during uncomfortable situations like Dale. I was fired numerous times from many radio jobs, and before each event, I was given countless opportunities to fix situations, but my inability to learn to cooperate prevented me from maturing.

We shop at a longtime family-owned grocery store called Festival Foods. Going there is a wonderful experience. Those who work there clearly love what they do. They are smiling and helpful and not afraid to share an optimistic greeting with us or provide help at any time.

Mark Skogan, a third-generation family owner of Festival, said this about getting people to work together: "We strive to hire associates who fit our culture. We call it hiring for attitude and training for skills. We cannot train attitude, so our hiring process is critical to finding associates who share our values."

And Charlene and I can tell you his company does this incredibly well. For more about Festival Foods and the inspiring story of this family and their business, I'd suggest you read the book by Mark's father, Dave, called, *Boomerang: Leadership Principles That Bring the Customer Back!*.

Getting along with people can be tough. I know one may rather have toothpicks lodged under their fingernails than to work with them, but we can certainly get better in that area. I'm certainly a work in progress in that space. If, by chance, anyone reading this has mastered the art of cooperation and is ever giving classes, please contact me immediately. The price of the tuition is irrelevant; I'll pay it. When the classes begin, I'll push for a front row seat, copiously taking notes. I wish I were kidding. I'm not.

## 6. The Principle of Communication

There are four forms of communication: reading, writing, listening, and speaking. As to the last, it's a fact that surveys have revealed there are some people whose number one fear is public speaking; they'd rather have a hot branding iron placed on their back than to say a few words before a crowd. One day, there was a man who was being put into a fenced-off area to be eaten by a lion. I think it was a pay-per-view event; I'm not sure. After introductions, the man was dragged into the arena, headed for certain death, and out of a door came the lion and the game was on—one that would have seemed to be one-sided!

For a few seconds, the combatants circled like a couple of boxers. Finally, the lion made a few ferocious lunges, missing the man, but not by much. But spectators noticed that every time the lion lunged past the man's head, the man would say something to the lion, and suddenly, the lion became very cautious and finally walked away from the man.

The man from the TV outlet hosting the event approached the man and began the interview.

"Sir, let's get right to the main question. How did you tame that hungry lion?"

"Well, actually, it was easy. All I did was let him know that after dinner, he would have to say a few words."

One of our trusted friends, who has presented with us at a Peanut Butter Promise Power Encouragement event, is co-founder of Culver's Restaurants, Craig Culver. You may have seen him in one of their positive television commercials. Their slogan is "Welcome to Delicious!"

With thousands of employees, the art of communication between employees and customers is, of course, imperative. Here is what Craig says on this issue: "My belief is that great communicators are, first and foremost, great listeners. Great communicators deliver their message with sincerity and energy, and it may not even have to be spoken. Being true to yourself and being true to your team members; transparency is the golden rule."

I do not consider myself an authority on the subject of communication. I am trying to learn to speak less and listen more. After all, God gave me two ears and only one mouth. A profound observation about speaking comes from Dr. Phil McGraw, the famous TV host who says, "Eighty percent of questions have an underlying statement to them." I wonder if that means I may be saying something else when I yell to the waiter, "Where's my mayo for my sandwich?" If the power of the Peanut Butter Promise would allow it, I'd like to ask Dr. Phil that personally someday.

Charlene and I always remind each other about the importance of thinking and sometimes rethinking before we push "send." Once we've done this, it is too late. This is an email analogy, but it also brings attention to my thick tongue and even harder head.

And once we have made this error, to try to draw it back is as hopeless as stuffing toothpaste back into a tube, or separating the Tang from water after you have stirred it in. A few words spoken in anger can prompt us to give one of the greatest speeches we'll ever regret. Sometimes it's best to just avoid situations that would provoke us to anger. As glad as I am for some of the things I have said, I'm more grateful for some I didn't say.

Good communication skills are needed in the sales field, and the best I know in that space is my dear friend Mike Janse. He is an award-winning sales account executive, another one of the all-time great communicators I have ever known. With great trust, I've listened to him transfer an idea to a client. Good communication like Mike is able to do is, in so many ways, the ability to be able to transfer a feeling to others. Pop used to tell me, "Minds are swayed by a truth well told," and it's our hope you'll find the truth in the Peanut Butter Promise, and it will set you free.

Even though I've been involved in the field of communication, I really do not believe I'm an authority on it. Like you, I'm trying to soak up as much as I can about this and other subjects. I can tell you that, for a long time, I wondered about the validity (and sanity) of positive self-talk, but I did come to the conclusion a while back that thinking nice things about myself is better than thinking bad things. And based on that, I've come to the conclusion that although communication with others is important, the most important conversation I'm a part of is the one I'm having with myself.

I would like to submit this quote I heard one Sunday while listening to a church service when the pastor said, "Keep your words soft and sweet, for you may have to eat them later." As for me, I'll be working on the art of proper communication until I am pushing daisies up under that tree where they will plant me and Charlene in Empire Cemetery. I mean it; I'm dead serious.

## 7. The Principle of Association

A guy was strolling the beach when he came upon a man fishing who had a bucket next to him. As the man drew closer, he saw the bait bucket had no lid and live crabs inside.

"Why don't you cover your bait bucket so the crabs won't escape?" he said to the man fishing.

"You don't understand," the man replied. "If there is one crab in the bucket, it would surely crawl out very quickly. However, when there are many crabs in the bucket, if one tries to crawl up the side, the others grab hold of it and pull it back down so it will share the same fate as the rest of them."

So it is with people and our associations. With this in mind, it would behoove us to take inventory of who the "crabs" are in our life. The moral of the story is: Get away from the crabs.

These individuals are the ones who are envious, those without your level of commitment and ambition. They proclaim, "If I can't have it, neither can you." Yeah, it's a perverted way of thinking for sure, but it is all too common, and this is why looking at the Principle of Association is so very important. It says we become who we spend time with.

The Bible, in Proverbs 13:20, says, "Walk with the wise and become wise; associate with fools and get in trouble." That's pretty clear. If we surround ourselves with wise people, we can become better. On the other hand, if we are spending time with people who have made poor decisions, we can become like them. I know this to be true, and truthfully, I've been more of the problem than the answer, but be assured I'm working on my stuff in this area.

From the arsenal of Zig Ziglar came this story. There was a farmer who owned an old, slow, dumb donkey. He was so disappointed with the animal's lack of ambition, and the creature's stubbornness annoyed him to no end. Then, he came up with an idea. He signed his mule up for the Kentucky Derby horse race. Of course, this perennial event featured many of the finest, swiftest thoroughbreds in the world. To no one's surprise, his beast finished dead last, coming in so far behind the winner, it was the first time in history that officials had to time a contestant with a calendar.

After the race, with no one left in the stands, the owner was asked a question by one of the curious media men still there.

"Sir, why did you put your donkey in the Kentucky Derby?"

The farmer said, "Because I thought the association would be good for him."

From that lesson, we learn that animals of a certain species and giftedness are limited, while human beings are not. They have in them the ability to improve their potentialities, and as referenced above, this is a very important fact of life. In a moment, we are going to propose three questions that align with this key principle. As important as it is to associate with the right people who can help guide us to where we desire to go, we are ultimately responsible for fulfilling our destiny.

In the old classic book from James Allen entitled *As a Man Thinketh*, he makes this point: "A man's weakness of strength, purity, and impurity are his own, not another man's. They are brought about by himself, not another, they can be altered by himself, not another." That said, it is imperative to associate with as many experts in your field that will help you on your arduous journey to fulfill your Peanut Butter Promise.

I've been very fortunate to have had association and communication with world leaders in the area of personal potential and growth. They've included Zig Ziglar, Brian Tracy, and Jim Rohn, and one of my greatest thrills was receiving a typed note of encouragement from the man I feel was the greatest media communicator of all time, Paul Harvey.

In his brilliant audio series, *The Art of Exceptional Living,* the late Jim Rohn notes there are two types of people with two types of stories. He notes that many are found in the Bible, those who served as either a warning or an example. Before Monday, April 15, 1991, there is no question that my life served as a warning.

In the next chapter, we will talk about the Law of Attraction, which is a cousin to this Principle of Association. Whereas our thoughts, behaviors, and choices attract people just like us into our lives, we become like those who we are with, which is important if we are going to find or continue on the path to fulfilling our purpose.

Here are three good questions to help work you through your personal and/or professional associations. There will be no test. Good luck.

**Who are the people I am spending time with, and what effect are they having on my life?** What do they have me thinking and doing? Am I rubbing off on them, or are they rubbing off on me? Are they taking me closer to or further from the achievement of my DreamGoals, the fulfillment of my purpose, and the Peanut Butter Promise?

**Of the people I am spending time with, who should I be spending more time with? Who should I be spending less or no time with?** Hint: They are the ones you should walk away from. They are the self-professed pessimists who can light up a room by leaving it. They are the ones with the crab mentality. They are the gossips, pretending to want your best but are surreptitiously moving pieces behind your back to see you defeated, just like them.

What people are not currently in my life that I would like to attract into my life that can help me fulfill my Peanut Butter Promise? These could include future Peanut Butter Promise Partners; we suggest that if you're seeking to become a Peanut Butter Promise Partner, you seek others that you feel are at that level you wish to go to, who have successfully done the things that you want to do.

As with everything else, it is imperative to be impeccably honest when answering these questions. Do remember always that we will become just like those we are with for any period of time. Why is it that we tend to catch "the sickness" of others rather than their "health?"

Like everything we have presented previously, it all needs to be chewed on for a bit before we decide whether we want to spit it out or swallow it, and let us promise you that Charlene and I choke on much of the Peanut Butter Promise too. You're not alone. If you will continue to keep trudging along on the journey to fulfill your purpose, you can count on us to be by your side. We're here to help you. We mean that sincerely.

That's a Peanut Butter Promise.

# CHAPTER 4

# 7 LAWS OF THE PEANUT BUTTER PROMISE

**W**hen we hear the word "law," some of us get a little uncomfortable, which may be an indication that we have a tendency to break a few of them. On one particular occasion, about seven months after the release of my first book, I looked into my rearview mirror to see flashing red lights. As the officer approached me, I was on my best behavior to avoid penalty. He spoke first.

"Good morning, sir. My name is Officer Hammen. Do you know why I am stopping you today?"

"No, not really," I confessed, knowing that I *may* have been traveling a bit fast for the local speed limitations.

"Well, sir, you were going forty-four miles per hour in a twenty-five mile-an-hour zone. May I see your driver's license?"

As I handed it out the window, he grasped it and said, "I'll be right back," and with that, he went back to his squad car.

I began to pray; that couldn't hurt, right?

As I saw Officer Hammen come back to my car, my heart began to beat a bit faster, actually a lot faster. He asked me a question, and after, I breathed a sigh of relief, sensing great mercy from the friendly policeman; also sensing my prayer was about to be answered.

"Say, are you the Steve Rose who wrote the book *Leap of Faith: God Must Be a Packer Fan?*"

"Yeah, that's me," I told him, and I was now more than 77.7 percent certain I was going to get off scot-free of my traffic crime.

"My goodness," he smiled. "I have a copy of the book. My mother has a copy, and I know a few friends have one too. Congratulations, Steve. It's a great book."

And then, what he said next was quite perplexing.

"Anyway, I'm sure with your status, schedule, and importance, you're very busy, so I will not keep you any longer."

I'm glad he realized what a big shot I was, that I was certainly in line for a pardon and would be given immediate release so I could go and continue to be important—so I thought.

"So anyway, Steve, *here* is your license, and *here* is your ticket for $107 for going forty-four miles an hour in a twenty-five mile-per-hour zone. Slow it down a bit. We need you and those around you safe so you can write more books! Have a great day, and God bless you for what you are doing. Keep up the great work!"

And with that, Officer Hammen strolled back to his car, entered, made a notation, and put his traffic signal on and drove away until he was out of my sight, seemingly never exceeding twenty-five miles per hour. I remained parked on the side of the road. It was then I had a little talk with the Lord. I asked him what just happened, and he explained. He reminded me of my own messages and sermons when I gave my deep take on the truth and consequences of the Law of Sowing and Reaping in Galatians 6:7.

It was then that I received the answer to my prayer. God spoke this into my spirit: *As you speed, so also shall you get a ticket.* Apparently, even big shot authors and speakers like me reap what we sow. Imagine that!

At times, we believe some laws are unnecessary. However, if we are truly growing as people, we finally come to the conclusion that laws are for our protection; they are bridges rather than walls. We discover upon faithful obedience that they are provided to guide us, and the same is true with the seven laws we will now share as part of the Peanut Butter Promise.

I heard a preacher say once, "We really do not *break* laws, but rather, when we violate them, they *break* us." That's maybe worth a reread, or at least a pause for meditation before proceeding to the author's forthcoming opinions on the subject.

This leads us to the seven laws of the Peanut Butter Promise. They feature unchanging universal, spiritual, emotional, mental, monetary, and physical truths that, when embraced and appropriately applied, pave the way for our personal accomplishments beyond what we could ever think or imagine.

The seven laws of the Peanut Butter Promise are: **Cause and Effect**, **Accumulation**, **Belief**, **Expectation**, **Attraction**, **Practice**, and **Impossible Substitution**.

Here goes.

## 1. The Law of Cause and Effect

On Tuesdays, I step on a scale. It never lies to me; it always tells me the truth—and that includes my dietary discipline for the seven days prior. The scale tells me the facts, much like looking in a mirror. It's hard to fool one of those as well.

The Law of Cause and Effect is like that; it's non-negotiable. It purports that our thinking leads to our feelings, and we act out of our feelings. In the classic writing by James Allen entitled *As a Man Thinketh*, he makes this bold statement: "Act is a blossom of thought, and joy and suffering are its fruits." If this is true, and the Peanut Butter Promise believes it is, this means thoughts are causes that lead to choices from which we take action; then, we get results, effects, and consequences. But he goes further: "Man thinks that thought can be kept silent, but it cannot; it quickly crystallizes into habit, and habit solidifies into circumstance."

If this law has a familiar ring to it, that would be because you may have heard about it in Sunday school or stumbled upon it in the Bible. Jesus of Nazareth called this concept the Law of Sowing and Reaping. Our neighbors, forever, have been the Rahns. Dave, his wife Sandy, and his brother Donny come over regularly to check up on us. They are wonderful people and great farmers, who, each year, plant the field right across the road from us.

Each spring, we watch from our deck how they prepare the soil for sowing (planting). This includes applying generous amounts of fertilization (that's cow manure). Then, they plant the seed in the field. We never know what they have planted until the plants come up. Finally, what has been planted pokes out of the soil. The past couple years, that has been corn.

And over the summer, we watch the corn grow. It is worth noting that the crop is sprayed with insecticide and other chemicals to keep the bugs and other enemies from preventing it from growing to its potential. But that's not enough. The crop needs ample amounts of sun and rain to make it grow. And finally, in the fall, if all has gone well, the crop is harvested, but not before it must go through the entire sowing and reaping process, which takes time.

Here are a few parallels to watching crops and people grow. First of all, the Rahns had to get out and plant the crop; they couldn't sit and watch television all day in the spring and expect a crop in the fall. Second, the seed they planted had to be good seed. The same is true for us; we must never expect a crop without planting, and for us, that can be reading or working on other parts of our character. Third, we cannot expect to be able to hasten the process. The same is true for us; there are no shortcuts in sowing and reaping.

One of the many great discoveries I encountered through the study of the great thinkers of personal growth and development is this: Our thoughts are things, and they lead us to take action, and thus, they produce results. This means that thoughts—seeds planted into our mind—result in actions and subsequently produce a harvest, which are our results.

Earlier, we discussed the benefit of choosing to display a positive attitude. However, a positive attitude, which is helpful, won't plant your garden. That's up to each one of us. And of course, we have to plant the right seed and pray for God's blessing to send rain and sunshine. Then, the farmer must maintain his machinery so he can harvest his crop and turn it into a profitable gain. It is a fact that life is a series of moment-by-moment choices we make today that affect our tomorrows, which include our short- and long-term DreamGoals and other objectives.

What we have gleaned from the Law of Cause and Effect is this: The very measure of our thoughts and study, from which we then choose to take action, will determine what comes back to us. Here's to you reaping a good harvest from the tree that does not lie, that has been planted in the garden of the Peanut Butter Promise.

## 2. The Law of Accumulation

We had a coffee maker that was very slow. It seemed to take forever to fulfill its purpose, which was to help us wake up and provide a bit of energy, or, for me, a cup of creativity to write. Drip by drip, it would labor as the heated water strained through the coffee grounds and drained into the pot. One of the lessons I learned was that watching the process did not speed it up one bit! But after a few minutes, and the longsuffering of my patience, there eventually was a pot of brew.

Another example might be the clock on the wall. The hands appear to never move, but minutes later, we find that they have. The same hours turn to full days, months, and years. Welcome to the Law of Accumulation, which says everything adds up over time. Further proof can be seen on our driver's license when we look at our age that reflects the unstoppable process of time, which some have said is our most precious commodity.

So how do we implement this law for our benefit? Actually, there are many ways, and the applications are unique to the reader who is truly serious about making the appropriate adjustments and taking the appropriate action.

An aspect of this law says that everything matters. Everything adds up, but just as we can slowly build, we can also decrease (and maybe that means the list of things to accomplish on a "To-Do" list.) Gabrielle Giffords said, "Mile by mile, it's a trial; yard, it's hard; but inch by inch, it's a cinch." If you were asked to eat an elephant, how would you do that?" The answer would be, "One bite at a time!"

If you're still having a hard time grasping what we're trying to say, maybe you could think about a closet or storage room. I've known some hoarders who seem to save everything. That doesn't start out as much, but after a few years, it all adds up by the Law of Accumulation. In some cases, this calls for a "tossing party," but if the law is calling for the gathering of something, maybe money, that would call for using the law to save.

Jim Rohn said both success and failure were related in this way. To be successful, all one must do is act daily in discipline and action over a long period of time. Conversely, to fail, all one needs to do is make a few errors in judgment daily over a long period of time.

Before we move on (and I don't want to brag—OK, maybe a little), let's go to the subject of money. Recently, our financial advisor told Charlene and me that we have enough money for the rest of our lives—that is, if we died seven months from today! So if you happen to enforce the Law of Accumulation and have too much, please send some to us!

## 3. The Law of Belief

I wound up, and with a great thrust, I threw my boomerang. I watched it gracefully swirl and twirl for about seven seconds. It seemed to change course, and as it came toward me, I wondered why it was getting bigger—and then it hit me. The revelation of why personal beliefs are critical to either the fulfillment, or lack of fulfillment, of my own Peanut Butter Promise happened in the same way.

Things are not always as they seem or look to be. In the '60s, there used to be breath spray in little bottles. One day, my brother Gary fired a couple squirts to the back of his throat. In two seconds, his face turned white, and he looked like he wanted to throw up. He looked at the can and on it read "Spray and Sparkle." It was not breath spray, but rather eye glass cleaner! Around the same time, my brother Dan was looking over some leftovers in the fridge. He spotted a brown concoction that looked like chocolate pudding. He took a few bites before he turned green and spit it out. What he assumed was pudding was gravy.

Now, it didn't matter what my brothers *believed* they were ingesting; they learned what the truth was, and the Law of Belief reminds us of this fact. In life, it is much of what we believe that creates the way we feel, and the way we feel determines the actions that produce our results. My father, David Rose, was, without rival, the greatest inspiration who provided a sufficient example of this philosophy.

I recall one day as we discussed the meaning of life, which was a large discussion. One thought that came up was that what we think and what we do ultimately lead us on our path for which we will be held accountable in the highest ways.

On this particular day, we agreed that truth is *not* relative, but truth is *truth*. We came to a conclusion that as humans, we can be deceived where truth is concerned. Further, Dad and I came to the mutual conclusion that quite possibly one of our most critical personal skills while on this earth may be narrowing the gap between what our opinions are and what the truth *really* is.

This is the gift to be able to differentiate truth from falsehood, a rare skill but much needed to win the tough game of life. I must confess that my biases and experiences did, and continue to, lead me to believe many things that may or may *not* be true. It's completely up to me, with God's holy help, to find out what truth really is in all things.

What truths have you accepted that could very well be lies? Let's say that I think gravity pulls upwards. Now, for most correctly thinking beings, that would seem preposterous, but to me, it is just one of my many goofy and potentially dangerous conclusions. Let's say I have been confronted by a person who knows the truth about gravity, but I remain in denial about it. So they ask if I would care to enter into an experiment that could clear up my confusion. Confident of my research, of course, I agree.

I am told to stand up on a table. It is approximately two-and-a-half feet above an uncompromising cold, hard, tile floor. It is then that I am told to fall forward. Under my firm belief that gravity will propel me upwards, I concur. I fall forward and bam! I have suddenly found the truth, or has the truth found me? It is then that I know the truth, and the truth may hopefully set me free. The first thing that must be set is my broken nose that's now smothered by a once pristinely white handkerchief.

Although I now may have learned a painful lesson of truth that has the ability to set me free in future decisions, it does not save me from the consequences of time, the expense of the doctor, dentist, and optometrist. Yes, my beliefs are very important. They have a tremendous impact on what I do or do not do. I need to be challenged by the second to know the facts so I can process my decisions properly and "Stop doing stupid!" For some of us, this takes longer than others.

I hope we have convinced you that our personal beliefs about all issues are important. As I learned in my double trip through Juneau, discussed in the Power of Plan and Action, it does *not* matter where we *believe* we're going but, rather, the true destination to where we're *really* headed. Stephen Covey cautions that we are best to make sure the ladder we are climbing is indeed leaning against the right building. Again, this has everything to do with correct and honest believing.

Why is the Law of Belief so very important and crucial to the fulfillment of our Peanut Butter Promise? One answer could be that where you are in your life right now is the very sum total of everything you have believed and, most importantly, acted upon up to this point in your life. And may I suggest that you monitor and test your beliefs? There was a time for me that I believed bathing my brain in a few cases of beer a week was good, which it wasn't.

Experts will tell us it's a fact that we will always act in accordance to our most dominant thoughts and beliefs. I personally believe that an ill-conceived perception eventually becomes a fully-believed reality.

The Peanut Butter Promise asks, *What beliefs do I hold as truths that may be wrong?* Once you have made your decision on a belief, take a stand for it, and act accordingly. Alexander Hamilton said, "If you do not stand for something, you'll fall for anything." It's one thing for us to be responsible for the bloody nose and broken teeth of our own dumb thinking, but let us never be found to have been the one who did the pushing. If you do, you'll not be able to help yourself, much less anyone else, come even closer to fulfilling their Peanut Butter Promise.

## 4. The Law of Expectation

The Peanut Butter Promise believes that many of our dreams and visions are a preview of our coming attractions, like when our dentist, Dr. Ruth Canal, takes x-rays of our teeth, especially the ones that need to be taken out. This is done so she can get a preview of coming extractions!

The Law of Expectation has the ability to show a preview of coming attractions to the truly dedicated and passionate Peanut Butter Promise Player. From my own experience, I can confirm that things we expect to happen can happen, but only if they are in agreement with our purpose. A crucial step is to get them down on paper, which we will help with in "The DreamGoal Achievement Program."

I firmly believe this law and the previous Law of Belief are very closely related; they travel along parallel paths. For the sake of this philosophy, we will assume, in most cases, that belief should precede expectation. One of the reasons is that we certainly need to have a solid belief we can achieve something before we can expect it to become a reality. When we expect something to happen, it will. Let us not forget to add one essential and often overlooked factor: Each assumption must be blended with sound faith.

I'm constantly amazed by the developments that occur while writing *The Peanut Butter Promise*. I just retrieved from the top of my bookcase a file that contained a notebook that held rapid-fire notes from 1994. I wrote the following wishes, some that were made real by first putting them down on paper as part of a DreamGoal sheet and pursuing them with an expectant and positive attitude.

They include the following:

- *TV Sports*
- *Be on* The 700 Club
- *Book (Write)*
- *Tapes – Self-Development/Testimony*
- *Do speeches*
- *Weight* (I have this original goal sheet from notebook too.)
- *1995 Town Car*

It's more than curious that some of these have come to pass, and by now, you can probably identify the ones that have. I like what Mike Utech said to us in 2015.

It was, "I bet you could buy a 1995 Town Car now pretty cheap."

He's probably right.

Timing can be everything in that our expectations must not arrive before their time, but it's fair to expect them to happen because if they are a part of your purpose, they will, and Peanut Butter Promise Players think and act that way all the days of their lives.

## 5. The Law of Attraction

There may be no other reason responsible for why you are reading these words at this moment than this law. It is mysterious, hope-laced, and intriguing. It asks this question: How did you come to read these words? And my answer would be by the Law of Attraction. And a better question would be this: Have we met for the greater good or detriment of each other and mankind?

The answer to that last question should give us great pause. The Peanut Butter Promise believes we attract both what is right with us and what is wrong. That notion is supported by James Allen, who, over a hundred years ago, wrote *As a Man Thinketh*. He made this comment: "Men do not attract what they *want*, but what they *are*." Wrap your thoughts around that line for a moment.

Further, it is the opinion of this philosophy that we are spiritual magnets that gravitate to or repel from one another for reasons not limited to those just mentioned.

It's been nearly thirty years, but the remembrance of being on a barstool occasionally comes to mind. In my self-created fog, I glance around me to capture a snapshot that I am in the presence of a few pretty nefarious-looking characters. But then, when I look in the mirror that hangs behind the bartender, it reveals that the drunk is me—all three of me!

I'm kidding about the people in the tavern, but not about seeing three of myself. I was told by my friend Brad—it was as true then as it is today—that if I wanted to get healthy and stay healthy, it was imperative for me to change my thinking and my environment to one conducive to the Peanut Butter Promise. I am so grateful I took this advice. He was right.

I'll go as far as to profess that the Law of Attraction chose my childhood friends and my teammates—that's right, even my teammates. As a young man, I used to watch a lot of softball, and there were two particular players I was especially fond of and attracted to.

One was a savvy shortstop I watched and admired in the early '70s. His name was Daryl Krug. He was a confident, slick fielder and a solid hitter, fast and smart. Another was John Bestor, who played for the Schlitz team in the mid '70s. Both of those guys were just like me: competitive. John had an afro haircut, and by my seventeenth year, I would have one just like him. Only a few years later, not by coincidence but by the very Law of Attraction, I got a call to play for Green Acres. I accepted and was on three championship teams from 1979 to 1981, and as a second baseman, I was right next to shortstop Daryl Krug. We were a pretty good double play combo. I just saw Daryl, who is still a great friend and wonderful person.

In 1980, I was scouted by a national championship level team, and was subsequently asked to play with them in the 1980 national slow pitch championship in Oklahoma City. The name of the team was Samantha's, but most intriguing was the man who scouted and invited me to play for them. It was none other than John Bestor!

Friend, neither of these two events were a coincidence, but they represent the very power of the Peanut Butter Promise and this law that plays no favorites. I invite you to go back and see how this law has played a role in your life. Just as it will draw people, it can draw opportunity, or just maybe attract you to a book. Hmm…maybe you're getting the idea?

I agree totally that our thoughts, wishes, and desires that line up with our purpose will come to pass. Just as I had to run from the barstool inside the brick and mortar of the bars I frequented, I had to escape their philosophies and attitudes. I think you get the idea. This law is a difference-maker, but don't take my word for it; read and study it.

## 6. The Law of Practice

What comes to mind when you think of the word practice? I'll go first. For me, I think of my lungs burning from wind sprints at one of Coach Hilgendorf's basketball practices. For you, maybe it's band, softball, or choir practices. Why is practice necessary? The Peanut Butter Promise philosophy proclaims it is so we can improve in many areas, but especially in the realm of our personal expertise that encompasses our talents, abilities, and gifts.

Before we would have you think this law is for physical practice, it is also a mental law that allows us, through repetition, to alter our thoughts. And for Peanut Butter Promise Progress, this would be adjusting our thoughts to be more positive and encouraging ones, rather than negative and discouraging ones. Let us remember from the Law of Cause and Effect that our thoughts, which are causes, lead to our behaviors, which lead to results, or effects.

The word that is most critical here is *habit*. It is practice, endless repetition, that creates our habits, whether favorable or to our detriment. Habits create our routines. We have both a conscious and a subconscious mind. I have learned that the conscious mind provides us with a choice, while the subconscious mind does not. The latter is playing a more significant role in our lives far beyond what we would ever know.

Speaking of the subconscious part of us, have you ever had a long day at work, and you were thinking about it as you cruised home through all kinds of traffic—maybe it was raining or snowing heavily? The travel required that you exit main highways and pass through numerous towns and villages, obeying numerous traffic lights and signs. Because of the nature of the journey, your mind was so far from realizing what you were actually doing, which was driving a metal missile at speeds of seventy-seven miles per hour.

This period of time on the road included hundreds of pumps on the brakes or the accelerator. You maybe even stopped for fuel, and you were totally engrossed in the moment. Finally, you arrived at your destination. Let me ask you this question. How much do you really remember about the traffic lights and the traffic around you? Possibly not much because your subconscious mind, by the mental Law of Practice, allowed you to do this. You were so enamored with the challenges at work and the like that your physical faculties were taken over by the Law of Practice.

Because I was an athlete who was able to compete at a pretty high level, I was privileged to be in the presence of a few souls who were pretty disciplined, having put hundreds and hundreds of hours of practice into their craft. I was fortunate enough to be able to squarely hit a baseball coming toward me at nearly a hundred miles an hour with a round bat. I was able to play racquetball at an open/professional level because of hundreds of hours on the court. I'm sure if you give it some thought, you'll realize you have equal skills.

As you watch any sport on television, this law cries out loudly. Look at the tennis player. How do they hit a ball a hundred miles an hour over a net and keep it on the court? A better question might be, how does the other guy return the serve and do the same?

For me, and I'm doing it as I write this, the greatest form for this law began nearly forty-five years ago, during my sophomore year of high school when I took a typing class. I have no idea how many keystrokes I have made today, but I confess I have a bit of a slight headache listening to music and even talking to Charlene as I type. And I would contend that it was this very skill, the Law of Practice, that could be the most responsible for writing this for you on the journey to fulfilling my purpose of the Peanut Butter Promise.

## 7. The Law of Impossible Substitution

As I drove down the driveway, I was certain that my lack of presence was going to take a toll on the massively positive production I had brought to Rose-E-Vue Dairy Farm. At least, I thought so, and at that time, that was all that mattered.

On September 14, 1981, I was leaving for my first full-time job in radio in Clarion, Iowa. Nearing the end of the driveway, I saw my father with his arm around my mom. It seemed both of them were crying, and I understood why. This was very much out of character, especially for my father, who typically kept a tough façade. I understood how and why this particular occasion had to have an element of devastation to it. After all, he was losing me on the farm. I'd assured them I would always be only a phone call away if they ever needed me, which, of course, was inevitable, right?

When I saw them weeping, I nearly turned around, but I resisted. I thought to myself, *No! I cannot go back. They are going to have to grow up on their own. If I continue to help them, they may always need and expect my help, and I will not always be here to help them!*

And so, with a toaster, frying pan, and hamper in my trunk, I resisted that temptation to return to the farm, and I drove the 357 miles to my destination. I will never forget (neither will my mom) when I called to ask her, "Mom, do you know how much a can of corn costs?"

I have to be honest. Something astonishing happened over the following month. Guess how many times my parents called me while I was gone to ask for my help or to bemoan of how much they missed me? Take your best approximate guess. The answer is none. Truth be known, it was *me* who spent the next month crying, living out of a suitcase in The Sandstone Motel, where, from its lonely confines, I missed my parents and family back home terribly.

A few weeks later, the wheels of my car may never have left the ground during what should have been a seven-hour trek. It took me only six. (I'm glad Officer Hammen was not following me. He probably couldn't have caught me anyway.)

Arriving home, I sped up the same driveway of the homestead of which I had departed only weeks before. I stopped my car near the barn. I saw my father coming from the barn to greet me. Unlike in the Parable of the Prodigal Son, he was not running. It was me who began to walk more briskly. I looked deeply into his eyes and shook his hand. Then, I revisited that emotional moment when I left four weeks prior.

"Dad, I cannot imagine how this time of growing has been for you and mother without me here. I noticed you were crying when I left, but I knew that maybe it would take the milk production to go down for you to totally appreciate me and learn some things you would not have learned with me here."

I couldn't understand why he was rolling his eyes. I continued.

"Dad, that moment when you saw me going on that journey of hundreds of miles to my dream must have been a tough moment for you and mother?"

And without hesitation, he spoke a hard truth to me. "Son, you don't understand. Those were tears of joy your mother and I were shedding."

Boy, I must admit, that kind of hurt. I had thought it would be nearly impossible to replace me on the farm. They would never be able to replace me—so I thought. That turned out to be true in this regard. The help they found after me was punctual, wrecked less machinery, and enjoyed farming a little more than I did. Let me reiterate: I loved growing up on the farm. It was the work I didn't like.

Has there ever been a time that you may have overestimated your worth? If you would go to the ocean and take out a bucket of water, do you think the level would go down? The answer to that is obvious, but it's still a fact that in the puzzle of the Peanut Butter Promise, you are important. As we told you in the first words of this book, you are impossible to replace! You know me a bit by now, and I'm not one to brag, but I did finish in the top 7 percent of the lower third of my class. I must confess I did get help to get out of school. While some graduate magna cum laude, I graduated "Thank the Lordy!"

One thing or pattern you may be noticing by now is that a few of the Powers, Principles, and Laws mesh together. I guess we could say they are interchangeable. While the Powers and Principles may have some wiggle room, the Peanut Butter Promise has found that if we can discipline ourselves, these Laws bring comfort because of their predictability, much like a Hallmark movie. Hang on—*nothing* is as predictable as one of those. We're not knocking the movies. As a matter fact, Charlene and I watch them regularly on popcorn date nights. In our opinion, the Hallmark channel is still one of the best channels on television.

The point is we can take some comfort in knowing that if we do something, we are guaranteed a certain result, and that may very well be the sermon the laws preach. The hard part is agreeing with them so you produce positive results rather than negative. That's easier said than done, but we're working on it, right?

As you are working through all the content the Peanut Butter Promise has presented thus far, let us never forget: This philosophy is a progress-not-perfection program. By Law of Accumulation, would you take just another step, turn the page, and move closer toward the fulfillment of your purpose? If so, we will remain right here by your side.

That's a Peanut Butter Promise.

# CHAPTER 5

# 7 VIRTUES OF THE PEANUT BUTTER PROMISE

A Sunday driver did the right thing, stopping at the cross-walk even though he could have beaten the red light by accelerating through the intersection. The tailgating woman behind him went ballistic. She pounded on her horn, screaming in frustration as she missed her chance to drive through the intersection all because of "Slow Joe" in front of her. Still mid-rant, she heard a tap on her window and looked up into the face of a very serious police officer.

"Ma'am, get out of the car." Once she did, he said, "Put your hands up. I'm going to take you to the police station," and that he did.

The woman was searched, fingerprinted, photographed, and placed in a cell. After a couple of hours, a policeman approached the cell and opened the door. She was escorted back to the booking desk, where the arresting officer was waiting with her personal effects.

He said, "I'm awfully sorry for this mistake. You see, I pulled up behind your car while you were blowing your horn, giving the guy in front of you an inappropriate gesture, and cussing a blue streak at him. It was then that I noticed your 'Choose Life' license plate holder, your 'What Would Jesus Do?' and 'Follow me to Sunday School' bumper stickers, and the chrome-plated Christian fish emblem on the trunk. Well, naturally, I assumed you had stolen the car."

Nobody likes hypocrites. It doesn't matter who we say we are or what we're going to do, actions do speak louder than words. We have already discussed this in the Power of Priorities, and we will continue in this vein throughout the book.

The Peanut Butter Promise defines a virtue as a godly behavior or personal character quality that can be deemed to be good. There are many things in life we *can't* change, but we *can* change our behavior and strengthen our character.

The seven virtues of the Peanut Butter Promise are: **Kindness**, **Compassion**, **Humility**, **Trustworthiness**, **Gratitude**, **Forgiveness**, and **Loyalty**.

The first is:

## 1. The Virtue of Kindness

A guy was asked, "Why don't you like shrimp and clams?" and his answer was, "Because they're so shellfish." And, like those, I can be pretty shellfish too—of course, I mean selfish. I'm learning moment by moment how to be more kind. We can *never* go wrong being kind to anyone at anytime. It doesn't cost anything, and it's one of those things expressed through words but even better in deed. Kindness can be expressed through good manners.

One person who has great manners is my mom. She always says, "please" and "thank you," which is not only appropriate, but kind.

My brother Jim learned a lesson about manners one day on a TV dinner Sunday when we were growing up in the '60s. He looked at my sister Gloria and made a very firm request.

"Gimme the milk."

She looked very patiently at him as he sat to her right, and then, she had a question for my brother.

"Pass the milk what?"

"Gimme the milk," Jim commanded, too proud to cave in and indulge my big sis with "the magic word."

"Pass the milk, what?"

And the showdown continued till, finally, my brother realized his antics were not getting him what he wanted.

"Give me the milk, please," he said to the amazement of all of us, never thinking he'd give in.

As Gloria was about to hand Jim the milk, my brother made a big mistake. He opened his mouth and said, "I take it back!"

Now, feeling she had been led on, mocked, and disrespected, she set out to give her brother a lesson he'd never forget (and frankly, neither would his four brothers at the table). Without another word, Gloria poured the whole pitcher of milk over Jim's head! I can still see that pure, white dairy fluid dripping from his face and off of his glasses. Jim always said please after that, and he's very kind today. So, what's the moral of the story? I guess to be sure to always say please to Gloria when asking for the milk!

I believe one of the truest tests of the character and kindness is how a company president or executive treats the janitor at his high place of business, or the cooks and wait staff in the company commissary. What we're trying to say may be best conveyed through this question. How do we treat people who may never be able to help us, or those we consider to be beneath us? The right answer will always be to be kind to them, not because it costs us nothing, but because it's the right thing to do.

Sometimes it's not always easy to receive gestures of kindness. In August of 2018, Mom and Pop's place was hit pretty hard by a tornado. It was a mess, but many hands make light work. One day, I looked out the door to find three teens with Kewaskum FFA T-shirts and gloves on. I knew exactly what they were up to, and I had to bury my pride.

"Oh man, at Campbellsport High school, we're taught not to like you guys!"

They laughed and revealed what we already knew they were here for.

"Can we help you clean up?"

"Of course, we'd appreciate that very much."

Those kids are going to go far for sure, especially Jada. A kindness like that is never forgotten—it can even land that person in a book.

One of the kindest people Charlene and I have ever met is John Schiek, who owns a wonderful world-leading brand called Schiek Sports. He should give classes on kindness. We hope you can meet him someday. Another is our friend Jon McGlocklin, former NBA player and broadcaster. He co-founded The MACC Fund in 1976. If you're looking for a charity to be kind to, look no further than them.

Speaking of kind and generous, my friend and racquetball doubles partner Mike Janse fits that bill. Jammer, thanks for all the kindness you have shown me over the years. The quality of kindness comes to mind when I think of my "Faithfull friend" Michael Van Dyck, Bill Breider from the Fox Cities YMCA, and Larry Pesch, a former basketball teammate who is such a friend to the Peanut Butter Promise, but even better, to Charlene and me.

## 2. The Virtue of Compassion

My mother Jean has had a pacemaker for over five years. I thank the person and team responsible for inventing it every day. Without it, my mom would not be here. Today's medical technology is fascinating. Although we take Mom in for heart examinations, the hospital is able to monitor her heart via the phone. Through this, they are able to tell when her heart is behaving in a way that it is not supposed to. One day, we received a call from the lady at the Pacemaker Clinic. Charlene answered.

"Hello, Roses!" she said cheerfully.

"Hi, this is Linda from the Pacemaker Clinic." She seemed very concerned, and that was reflected in this question. "We were wondering if there was anything unusual that happened with Jean at about two p.m. on Saturday, April ninth."

Charlene pulled the phone down and told me what she said, and a light bulb went on. That was when we told her that her granddaughter Sandi had died unexpectantly. That solved the mystery of the out-of-whack heart pattern. The machine at the Pacemaker Clinic noticed that my mother's heart had received a blow in that moment. Thankfully, my mom rebounded from that news, and we were able to be there to comfort her at the time.

Like our mother in that moment, there are times when we all need compassion and when we need to be there to give it to others, but most humans are not hooked up to a machine that announces to those around them they need it. I've known about compassion for many years. I *think* I know what it means, but do I *really*? *The Oxford Dictionary* says it is "the feeling of sorrow for the suffering of others." If we're paying any kind of attention at all, we will notice that people around us are suffering in one way or another. It seems we're all going through *something*, but the *something* of the other person, as we just pointed out, is not always known and, in some cases, is none of our business.

The Peanut Butter Promise point we are trying to make is that if we are honest, we should all come to the conclusion that we need to be more compassionate toward our fellow man. There are various reasons why we do not show ample amounts of compassion. I'll go first. I can be so self-absorbed in my own life that I am not paying attention to those around me who may have just learned they have a deadly disease—the same goes for a friend or colleague. Another reason is that I cannot relate to the pain or struggle of the other person, which is really no excuse.

Until last year, I did not know the pain of the loss of a loved one, but now I do, and I am more equipped to stand in to comfort those who need it because of this loss. I still have far too many areas where I need to be more aware. I can tell you in terms of money issues, specifically the lack of it and the consequences of irresponsible squandering, I'm there. When someone talks about divorce, I'm there. It wasn't until recently, but I can now relate to those who have gotten a personal voicemail from their doctor informing them to call them back at their earliest convenience. It's paying attention, or having the ability to relate to someone whose shoes you have walked in.

I treasure my lifelong friend Bill Grady, who I will always love, just as I do my brothers. He showed compassion to me during some of the lowest times in my life, mainly because of what the Peanut

Butter Promise calls The Power of the Common Experience. What I mean by that is he's gone through many of the same experiences, both high and low. People like Bill know the importance of providing an ear to anyone who needs it at any time of the day.

A seven-year-old young girl learned that a neighboring man of about eighty had recently lost his wife. Seeing the man sitting on his porch rocking in his chair, sullen, with eyes looking mostly straight ahead, occasional tears streaming down his cheeks, the young lady would go over and sit with the grieving widower.

When asked by her mother what she would say to the hurting man, she replied, "Sometimes nothing. Most of the time, I just sit on his lap and cry with him."

Yes, sometimes our neighbors just need someone to cry with. It's not always necessary to speak.

## 3. The Virtue of Humility

I've had some wins and losses in the area of humility. I can tell you that I learned during the writing of this book that it's easier to be humble when, at fifty-nine years old, you need to wear a diaper. Keep reading, and we'll share the whole story.

A friend that comes to mind when I think about the wonderful quality of humility is Dick Bennett, who was the head coach of the 2000 Wisconsin Badgers basketball team that went to the Final Four. And the apple does not fall far from the tree with his son, Tony, coach of the NCAA 2019 University of Virginia Cavaliers. I do not know Tony, but I hope through prayer and the power of the Peanut Butter Promise I may be able to meet him someday.

One Sunday, Pastor Pete Koeshall, a very sweet-spirited and wise man, had just finished an outstanding message about humility. You may not believe me when I say I *was* paying *close* attention and taking copious notes. Pastor reached down behind his podium and came up holding a huge bag of diapers. He made his way down the area near the front rows, where he made an offer.

"If there is a new mom, one who could use some diapers, I invite you to come forward and take them home with you."

Over the following four seconds of silence, you could have heard a Kimberly-Clark Huggies diaper hit the carpet. And then, a young lady of about twenty-five stepped out from a pew near the back of the church. With every eye upon her, she made her way to the front. When she arrived into Pastor's presence, he gave her a comforting hug knowing the courage it took for this woman to come forward. He then looked at the congregation and gave this sermon.

"If we can humble ourselves and receive a gift, sometimes there is more to that gift than we know."

Then, Pastor reached to the bottom of the diapers and pulled off a hundred dollar bill he had attached to it. He handed the diapers and the bill to the woman, hugged her one more time, and the grateful new mom wept on her way back to her seat. The Bible says, "For those who exalt themselves will be humbled, and those who humble themselves will be exalted." (Matthew 23:12)

Humility, the quality of being able to be humble, is the ability to not think too high or low about our self. This is easier said than done, and it's probably no surprise to you that it has much to do with what is happening in our lives at any given time. The opposite of humility could be conceit, which is when a person has an overblown positive opinion of themselves. Conceit is a gift from the devil to the self-absorbed person. You know, it's that guy who,when he speaks about himself for minutes on end, you do everything you can to keep from projectile vomiting.

In his books, (and most recently, he repeated it to me in his audio album *Personal Excellence*) bestselling author Ken Blanchard said it this way. "Humble people don't think less of themselves, they just think of themselves less." That's a great bar for me to try to reach for, as I'm far from there.

I've learned that, in life, it is very important to never allow myself to get too high or too low emotionally. It's about keeping balance. For me, that will be an eternal struggle, and I'm OK with that. It's a fact that happy people are humble people; they know the world does *not* revolve around them. They have come to the conclusion that, like you and me, they need Peanut Butter Promise Partners.

One humble man who helped me change my life forever is Peanut Butter Promise Partner, Ken Ruettgers, this six-foot-six, 277-pound teddy bear, a guy who played offensive tackle in Green Bay protecting a guy name Brett Favre. It was Ken who helped me get our first message through the book *Leap of Faith: God Must Be a Packer Fan*. Ken, for that, I will always be so very grateful.

There are benefits of humility. They can be spiritually, mentally, emotionally, and even physically. Humility, or the lack of it, can be the source of material, financial, and other kinds of wealth. It can lead to blessings if we are willing to surrender and not be overly self-conscious. Be assured that *life* has humbled me. I have been thrown many times by myself off the pedestal, upon which I, and I alone, had placed myself.

That's not to say I don't feel good about myself and who I am. I still think I'm pretty important. As a matter of fact, I still make offers at the local mall and grocery store to sign autographs, mostly in the checkout lines. The awkward part is when I have to explain who I am. I hope that will change if I see you in aisle seven by the peanut butter and jelly at Festival Foods.

Speaking of humble people, I'm so grateful that Charlene and I ran into our friend, Mark Reimer, at Festival during the writing of this book. His picture should be right next to the definition of the word "humble" in the dictionary. He's a wonderful man and a dear friend to us.

If we take a look at those people who make us feel good about who we are, they are secure and humble people, and we should strive for this virtue to be downloaded into us so the odds of fulfilling our Peanut Butter Promise may increase in leaps and bounds.

## 4. The Virtue of Trustworthiness

When Mom and Dad needed a new bathroom to better take care of their needs, we called Mike Braatz to come and head up the project. Because our family had a longtime trusting relationship with Mike's father, it was an easy decision to have Mike help. Not only did he help, but he brought Don Schmidt, a plumber, and another person into the project. Shortly after came Floyd's drywall, and so on and so forth. The bathroom looks beautiful, especially Mike's cabinets. He, like his dad, is a real craftsman. Trust is very important.

Trust that when we have the gift of trust from others, we have *everything*. When we've lost it, we have *nothing*. For the sake of this writing, we are calling this virtue trustworthiness. Ask yourself: What is the most important part of a relationship, personal, business, or otherwise? What would you say? For me, that is trust. Having and giving trust is so very, very important, but we must learn to tread and trust carefully. It cannot be given randomly and must be earned. And a key element where it is concerned is time but, more importantly, truth. Upon closer review, we notice the very root of the word *trust* are the three letters, t-r-u, the same ones in the word truth, which is also an essential component to giving and receiving trust.

A good question for me is this. Is what I am doing in my relationships trust-building or trust-burning? I'm fortunate to have earned a good supply of trust from family, friends, and business associates. I also regret that I have caused the loss of trust in a few people, and I take total responsibility for that. I'd guess that if a person has a handful of people on the planet they can trust, that would be generous. I have a few Peanut Butter Promise Partners I put into that category.

I have learned, and maybe you have as well, that it can take a long time, sometimes years, to build trust in a relationship. Like the sink in The Principle of Integrity, it can be lost in an instant. Yes, trust is like that. Here today, gone tomorrow. It is a precious thing to have and to give. We must give great discretion in where and with whom we can confide in—who will keep our failures safe, and possibly our joys even safer.

Benjamin Franklin said, "Two people can keep a secret if one of them is dead." That is sad commentary for sure. It's a truth that many of us have suffered much regret when we have failed someone's trust. On that note, it would certainly behoove us to make the art of giving and receiving trust from the right people one of our highest priorities. Like the trust-building process, it can take a bit of time.

## 5. The Virtue of Gratitude

What if I were to tell you I woke up with a sore throat, but oh, it got worse from there. Then, I learned that Charlene had somehow lost one of her seven diamond necklaces. And if it couldn't get worse, my Mercedes-Benz automobile would not start. When I went into the house to share this with Charlene, she told me she just got off the phone with not only the maid but the butler too, and neither of them were going to be able to come and take care of us. If I called you and told you this story, how would you receive it? Yeah, that's what I thought; you'd think I was not grateful, and you'd be right.

Very few things in life are cut and dry, black and white, but I'll venture with the greatest of confidence that a major determinant between a sad or a joyful person is gratitude. It should be no secret to you by now that the Peanut Butter Promise philosophy professes that being happy or disgruntled is a choice. This is not to say there are not times that warrant anger and grief but, rather, that our attitudes are a reflection of our past and present decisions.

This is a good time to provide a reminder of the Peanut Butter Promise definition of success. It is living with an attitude of gratitude while keeping our priorities in order and integrity intact, using our talents, abilities, and gifts to serve others as we fulfill our purpose. It is the first portion of this sentence that shares what we believe is at the very heart of being successful, and it's a choice! That's right; being truly successful can be just a choice away!

I believe a great attitude is a result of being grateful. Let's settle on having a great attitude, which is to be prayerfully optimistic but realistic in all things. If we take a closer look at the people around us who are smiling, we can see they are grateful people. What about the ones who are frowning? I contend that many of them have an attitude of entitlement, and this disease, in my humble-but-deadly-accurate opinion, can be fatal.

Not fatal in that you could die. No, much worse. You can go through life with this flawed thinking, being miserable, envious, jealous, and totally insecure, believing the world owes you everything, looking to grab a carrot that can never be caught. I assure you those who suffer from this mentality are hard-headed and hard-hearted fools. Sorry to be this blunt, but if you do your own studying, I think you'll find the same thing.

A morning does not begin or night end in our home when Charlene and I do not thank the Lord for what we have. And our lists are different. For me, at times, I will blurt my gratitude for a garage because, for many years, I had to go out to a dead battery or move my car (which sometimes wouldn't start) so the apartment parking lot could be plowed. While taking a shower, it is not unusual to hear my wife professing out loud, "Thank you, Lord, for hot water and indoor plumbing."

You see, she once had her water turned off, and she had to boil water that originated from a snowbank, so that is something she was, and remains, very grateful for. And I should be too. I'm old enough to remember when we had an outhouse because the indoor toilet was not always reliable. A stinky subject, just like the stinking thinking related to a bad attitude that can take a person right to the bottom of the pile at the bottom of the outhouse.

When Charlene and I think about gratitude, a face comes to mind. It is of our friend Kostas Katris, who came to the United States from Greece many years ago. He is a restaurant owner who understands the blessing of not only living in the United States, but is equally as grateful to own a business here. Because of that, he is always content.

During the national COVID-19 pandemic, I was watching infectious-optimism preacher Joel Osteen on a national cable show, where he was reminding the audience that despite what was happening, we all had things to be grateful for. He was presented this question by the host.

"How, in this kind of situation, can you tell someone who has lost their job or maybe a family member to be grateful?"

Joel answered, "I understand that, but we all have things we can be grateful for in any situation. If you have a house in which to live, a car to drive, and friends, those things are very important."

Charlene and I pray every day in thanks that we live in a house that when it is cold, we can make it warm, and when it is warm, we can make it cool. That we have not one, but two cars, that we have our health. We have learned that being grateful is a real key to opening the door to blessings. We also understand that there are times we go through difficult things, but it is always the right thing to "count your blessings" and remember that there is always someone who has it worse than you do.

On the subject, we have found it is also very important to be grateful for what you have while you're waiting for what you want, with the reminder to live and learn in today. The past is history, tomorrow is a mystery. Today is a gift; that's why it's called the present.

## 6. The Virtue of Forgiveness

If you have been breathing for any period of time and are conscious, you have probably been wronged—some of you more than others.

I'll confess that one of the most prominent messages that challenges me is that of forgiveness, not so much receiving it but giving it. When the time and need comes for me to show forgiveness, I can be at my worst. As a matter of fact, I'd sooner wish a tribe of 7.7 million hungry mosquitoes to swarm, enter the offender's home, and feast on them forever, rather than forgive them. But I must forgive them.

Let me make it very clear that there has never been anything that anyone has ever done to me that has been so deeply hurtful that I cannot give forgiveness freely. I know some of you who are reading this have had things done to you in the past, or even currently, that are unimaginable to some of us. Let me be clear, I am not telling you what you should do here. Some of your wounds will require much counseling, and a counselor I am not. Truth be told, I'm not even a really good writer—I simply provide some ideas—but I do know forgiveness is a key to fulfilling your Peanut Butter Promise purpose.

I'd like to share a couple stories of forgiveness that come from close relatives and, because of that, were a part of my experience. On the evening of Friday, March 20, 1985, Pastor Balken knocked on the door of my Uncle Norb and Aunt Joyce. It was as if he was walking into a nightmare. On this horrible occasion, it was to inform them that their twenty-year-old daughter Paula had been murdered. Of course, the parents were stunned, and if they had been furious forever at the person who committed the act, anyone could have understood that.

What my Uncle Norb did over the next few days was astounding. I, personally, will never forget as a lost, twenty-five-year-old alcoholic, listening at Paula's funeral as Pastor shared a letter from Paula's father forgiving the person who had murdered his daughter.

My uncle and godfather had a wonderful testimony he never missed an opportunity to share until his heaven-going in 2010. By now, you probably have an idea what kind of man he was and the wonderful legacy and challenge for us to forgive that he left behind.

In 1982, three years prior to Paula's murder, I was doing radio in Iowa. One morning, I received a call from my mother. She informed me that my first cousin Bobby, who was a thirty-four-year-old, eight-year sheriff's deputy in Sarasota County, Florida, had been killed in a terrible car crash by a drunk disbarred lawyer. The man had survived the accident but was on life support. Bobby was the only son of my Aunt Viv and Uncle Bob. Upon receiving the news, they made arrangements to travel from their home in the Midwest to Florida to receive his bride who had just given birth to a son named Andrew.

Knowing the guy who had so irresponsibly participated in the sudden, tragic loss of his son, Uncle Bob understandably planned to go right from the airport to the hospital, enter his room, and pull every plug that was keeping him alive! It would make sense that this would even the score, right? Thankfully, he thought better of that and began to cope and enter the tumultuous steps of grief.

Ironically, it was a man by the name of Father Faith who presided over Bobby's state funeral that included hundreds of Florida state troopers. There were also other Florida state police agencies in the procession, even a state trooper from Wisconsin, his home state where he had previously served. And with the Good Lord and Father Faith's guidance, my aunt and uncle survived the ordeal, but make no mistake, their lives were altered drastically. My aunt died two years ago, and as of this writing, my Uncle Bob, one of the finest people I have ever met, is still alive and living on his own at ninety-five. (As a footnote, the man on life support did die shortly after the accident from his injuries.)

The experts will assure us that if we do not forgive those who have harmed us, those feelings will fester, grow muscles, and continue to pound us into submission. William Ward said, "Forgiveness is the key that unlocks the handcuffs of hate." Yes, this is just another area where it's easier said than done. But for me, it's important for me to seek the courage to ask for forgiveness (where appropriate) from those I have hurt and continue to forgive those who hurt me and have, in some cases, continued to hurt me, but I pray for them, love, and forgive them as God has forgiven me. Amen.

## 7. The Virtue of Loyalty

We all need people who are loyal to us, and we need to provide the same. Loyalty is a strong sense of support or allegiance, which can be for a clothing brand, restaurant, or sports team. However, for this purpose, we will say it concerns people. We are loyal to those we trust, and we trust those who are loyal to us. Like the virtue of trustworthiness we explored and expounded upon earlier, we are talking about the element of *time*. It takes good shares of time to earn and give loyalties, but unfortunately, not much to lose them.

There is a lot of talk about loyalty in the corporate sector and, specifically, about one's loyalty to his company. I would like to give this commentary about that. Loyalty to your employer, boss, and coworkers is very important, but to me, only to the degree of how you are being treated, with an emphasis on compensation. What I am trying to say is loyalty in the workplace needs to only go as far as fairness and the degree to which you can help your family.

For sure, when Charlene and I think about loyalty, we think of a few of those close to us. One is Mike Utech; another is my brother Dale. I will add my brother-in-love Randy to this list. He is a wonderful, humble man whom I can trust with my whole heart. All these angels have proven to be loyal to us and everything we do, and we plan to give back the same to them. We have learned loyalties must be given freely after trust is earned. This is many of the wonders. We cannot project fear on others to obtain or keep them, and this is most apparent in a marriage.

As I ponder loyalty and those who have been loyal to me, I see the face of my brother-in-love Randy and his wife, my favorite big sister Gloria. OK, she is my only big sister Gloria. Outside of my dear Charlene and brother Dale, truer faces, arms, and hearts of loyalty I may never see.

One of the most touching stories of loyalty I have ever encountered comes from the battlefield. I'd like to dedicate it to Randy, who has served his country (in Vietnam), his family, his friends, and God very well. The story tells of how horror gripped the heart of a World War I soldier as he saw his lifelong friend fall in battle. Caught in a trench with continuous gunfire whizzing over his head, the soldier asked his lieutenant if he might go out into the "no man's land" between the trenches to bring his fallen comrade back.

"You can go," said the lieutenant, "but I don't think it will be worth it. Your friend is probably dead, and you may throw your life away."

The lieutenant's advice didn't matter, and the soldier went anyway. Miraculously, he managed to reach his friend, hoist him onto his shoulder, and bring him back to their company's trench. As the two of them tumbled in together to the bottom of the trench, the officer checked the wounded soldier and looked kindly at his friend.

"I told you it wouldn't be worth it," he said. "Your friend is dead, and you are mortally wounded."

"It was worth it, though, sir," said the soldier.

"What do you mean worth it?" responded the lieutenant. "Your friend is dead."

"Yes, sir," the private answered. "But it was worth it because when I got to him, he was still alive, and I had the satisfaction of hearing him saying, 'Jim, I knew you'd come.'"

I hope you will find the courage to practice each of these virtues: Be more kind, compassionate, and humble; become more trustworthy; be more grateful, forgiving, and loyal. Because if you can, and will, I assure you that you will find and remain on the very path that leads to the fulfillment of your purpose. If you do, it's not a matter of *if*, but *when*, you will.

And *that*, my friend, as always comes with a Peanut Butter Promise.

# CHAPTER 6

# THE DREAMGOAL ACHIEVEMENT PROGRAM

**E**ighteen-year-old Joey had worked two years for the Barnum and Bailey Circus. His job was to follow close behind the elephants—actually very close behind—with a shovel. This was because, well, when the elephants had to "eliminate," the contents didn't fall to the ground, but onto his shovel. It didn't always work out, but Joey had gotten to be pretty good at, uh, well, whatever it was called that he was doing. He loved the job, the people, the whole works. Although the unique occupation had its issues, he was a team player.

After returning home to his family for a few days of well-deserved rest, he was with his father who asked him a question.

"Son, when are you going to get a 'real job'?"

Perplexed, Joey answered back, "What do you mean by a 'real job'?"

"Well," trying to be as tactful as possible, his father said, "you know, maybe for the railroad or in the manufacturing sector, where you may have a bit more prestige and be able to make more money?"

Joey thought about that for a second, and then answered his father with, "You mean, leave show business?"

There's a difference between what we want to be doing and what we should be doing, and The DreamGoal Achievement Program can help guide you through the process of maximizing your talents, abilities, gifts, and time. It is a proven system that involves identifying wishes and then turning them into DreamGoals when we put them down on paper and pursue them with a plan and action.

Like the maps we discussed in the Power of Plan and Action in "7 Powers of the Peanut Butter Promise," DreamGoals serve as a blueprint and a map to what we want to accomplish. The Peanut Butter Promise DreamGoal Achievement Program comes with a guarantee. It is this: "It *will* work, but only if *you* do!" You knew you'd have to work for what you are looking to attain, right?

The seven DreamGoal categories of the Peanut Butter Promise are: **Faith**, **Family**, **Friends**, **Financial**, **Career**, **Health**, and **Personal**.

Let's begin with the first that, in my opinion, is the most important.

## 1. Faith

I'm always flabbergasted when I am watching a baseball game and see a fan catch a foul ball—with a baseball glove! Think about this for a second. Someone had the faith to take their mitt, planted along with thirty thousand other fanatics in the ballpark. So, the chances are one in thirty thousand, right? And they accomplished their goal. We should all have such a baseball-glove-type faith. That would be identifying faith as a verb.

Now, let's discuss faith as a noun—in this case, a belief in God. Before we go further, you may ask, "Do I need to believe in God to enjoy the many benefits of the Peanut Butter Promise?" The answer to that is "no." The benefits of the philosophy can be enjoyed by those who employ the ideas of it. As for Charlene and me, we are Christians—followers of Jesus Christ—and to be clear, our mission and the message of this book is not to convert you. That said, we would not be true to ourselves and the message if we didn't share this fact, and we're always willing to talk about it with anyone who asks.

We do believe the following about God: He has fearfully and wonderfully made us having thought of everything we need. Imagine if, as human beings, we were created without a big toe. It would be rather hard to stand, wouldn't it? How about if you didn't have an elbow? It would be kind of hard to eat, wouldn't it? What if the greatest quarterback in the world, Aaron Rodgers, didn't have a wrist? That would make it very difficult for him to cock his arm, bend his elbow, snap his wrist, and throw one of those touchdown passes at Lambeau Field, wouldn't it?

One of the great benefits for Charlene and me is that as we follow God's lead, He will guide us—and truth be known, we've asked for His guidance in every keystroke of what we pray is faith-building for you. I think you get the point. Every part of us is special and needed, and so are you. The Peanut Butter Promise believes we're each born with a divine seed in us that has the potential to grow and yield a crop that can feed many people—you and many others. Amen.

An example of a Faith DreamGoal is coming up in the DreamGoal Wish List.

## 2. Family

You cannot pick your family—you get what you get—and they just have to put up with you, and for that, I'm grateful to mine who put up with me. The Peanut Butter Promise promotes that for this section, we will put our spouse (if applicable, of course) as the highest aspect of family.

Although Charlene and I are surrounded with siblings, we put the loving and nurturing of each other first after our faith, then our children and grandchildren, then our brothers and sisters, etc. The greatest example of selfless love and service to family is Charlene. I've watched her spend countless hours helping her sister Lynn during her eighteen-month battle with cancer. Today, she is still taking care of family. Stay tuned.

Now, you may say, "But Steve, you just proclaimed that faith should be our top priority!" Well, that depends on the situation. Let me give you a recent example. Charlene, my mother, and I were in the midst of our morning devotional time when my phone rang. Caller ID showed it was my brother Dan.

"Brother Daniel!" I answered.

"Yeah, Steve, I ran out of gas with the four-wheeler back by the marsh. Can you bring me some gas?"

Now, that brought about a need for what we will call the Peanut Butter Promise "DreamGoal Priority Purifier." Because we were right smack dab in the middle of reading scripture, I could have said, "Well, Dan, too bad. We are in the middle of our Bible reading, and you know faith is our top priority around here; I cannot come. Sorry." And I could have hung up on him.

I could have said that, but my brother Dan needed to be made a priority in that situation. He's always been there for me, but even if he hadn't. So, after percolating the data through the "DreamGoal Achievement Priority Purifier," we determined that the right thing to do was to drop everything and go help Dan.

Imagine if the Good Samaritan (remember that one from Sunday school?) had told the man beat up on the side of the road, "Gee, pal, I'd really like to help you, but you see, I'm on my way to church. As a matter of fact, I'm running late. When I get there, I have to prepare the communion trays, and I missed choir practice, so I have to get in a few verses of 'Amazing Grace' that we'll be singing."

The point is if the Good Samaritan hadn't helped, he would have been a hypocrite—and when I sit in church that means there's one more, but I'm working on my stuff, believe me. It certainly helps our credibility when our actions are congruent with our words. In other words, we have to practice what we preach. What a concept.

Also see the Golden Rule that says, "Do unto others as you would want them to do unto you." In other words, help your brother when he's out of gas and he'll help you when you need it. Take care of family whenever you can. You'll never, ever regret it.

## 3. Friends

Friends are supposed to be, well, friendly. Unlike family, you can pick your friends, and it can be a trial and error process. In this process, you will want to be careful. We all have a side to us we don't want to show, and to that, I plead guilty. When Charlene and I go to

Los Angeles on business, we also see our friends, Michael Van Dyck, Justin Pierce, Simran Singh, and Seth Zieliecke.

One of our favorite things to do is go to Sony Pictures Studios, where Justin will take us to a taping of *Jeopardy* or *Wheel of Fortune*. Another thing Charlene and I love to do at Universal Studios is visit the locations, sets, and soundstages where many of the movies and television shows you've seen are filmed. On one of the tours on the streets there, you will see a street with buildings. But after you get closer to the structures, you notice something very peculiar and unnoticeable from only one view. It is the fact the buildings are nothing more than a seven-inch façade made of wood! Certain people can be like that too. They, like me, can put up a façade, hiding what's really behind them. So be careful when picking your friends, knowing that one of the heartbreaks of life is going through those times when you "find out who your true friends are."

If you are fortunate enough to have a few friends, congratulations, you're blessed beyond measure. I'd like to talk about one of my lifelong, dear friends. I talked briefly about him earlier. He is Keith Fryman. We've been pals for over forty-five years. We've been through a lot together. A few of our major accomplishments were sitting through back-to-back-to-back nights of watching the movie *American Graffiti*. It didn't stop there. We did the same with *Young Frankenstein* and *Airplane*.

As a matter of fact, at any time, any minute or hour of the day, I can send Keith a one-liner from any of those movies, and within a few seconds, he replies with another one. He actually just sent one as I was writing this. I'm serious. Everyone should have a friend like Keith, one who sticks closer than a brother. We're connected spiritually in a wonderful way, so much so that I believe if neither of us could talk or hear, we could still hold a very meaningful conversion. And to that point, I am also serious. And the unique chat would include a lot of laughing—and lines from those three movies!

My friend of thirty-plus years, our right hand man, Mike Utech, is as faithful as they come. If it weren't for him hearing of my need for a computer to write my first book in 1996, no one, including you, would be reading this right now. I wonder if we still have that floppy disk somewhere. In my life, Mike has been irreplaceable. When my world has blown up, and it has more than once, he's been there to help pick up the pieces without judgment. When everyone else was "running out," he was "running in." To this day, he holds the ladder on which we are climbing, and he does it all quietly, behind the scenes, needing no fanfare. He's also got the best stories about me, and you are free to ask him about any of them. We trust him that much. Thanks, Mike.

One of the most chilling lines about the importance of friendship comes from the classic movie *It's a Wonderful Life*. At the end, Clarence the angel writes a note in a book to George Bailey: "Dear, George. Remember, no man is a failure who has friends."

The crux of what we're trying to communicate here is that friends are important and should be put into the proper line of priorities. And you should set a DreamGoal or two of how to attain and keep a few.

## 4. Financial

There was a song in the '70s that went, "Money, money, money, money…money!" In the world we live in, you'd think money is important, and to that, we say, "It *is*!" As Zig Ziglar used to say,

"Anybody who says money isn't important, well, I'd guess they'd probably lie about other things that are important too!" He'd then proclaim that money is right up there with oxygen.

Some people say money is not important and that it can't make you happy. Knowing it takes money to eat and pay bills, why do some people say such things? After some reflection, I believe those who make such statements are quite possibly envious of those who possess plenty of cash, resources, and possessions. They are either too lazy or have no idea how to obtain these things morally and ethically, or they are the ones who have not learned how to have a disciplined spending budget nor feel the need to. Because of this, they throw their money away as if they can print more. Then, they have the audacity to blame others for why they don't have any and plead to get some from those who have it.

The misinformed say money is evil. It's not money that's evil. Scriptures say, "The *love* of money is the root of all evil." Did you catch that? It's not *money* that's evil, but the *love* of it and how you obtain it. Keep this fact in mind. Money is nebulous, neutral. It is emotionless, with no motives. Those are held by the one holding it. A wise man I know said something like the following, and the Peanut Butter Promise agrees: "It is not bad to have things or possessions, but it is certainly a tragedy when those things possess us."

And it's OK to have money. I love what Pastor Rick Warren said when questioned by a pompous host during a cable television interview. The verbose and pious man behind the microphone couldn't resist castigating Reverend Warren when he asked this question.

"Pastor Warren, do you think it is a sin to be rich?"

And without hesitation, he said, "No, but I think it's a sin to die rich."

What a great lesson on money. And by the way, it's fascinating that the person doing the interview wouldn't have necessarily qualified for food stamps either.

We say again, money is important, very important, especially when we need to eat, pay the mortgage or rent, buy clothing, pay other bills, or help those who cannot help themselves. Other than that, it's no big deal, right? The ignorant couple says, "Well, we don't have much money, but we have a lot of love." I wonder how that plays out when the bank calls reminding the happy couple that their house payment is three months in arrears. (That's a fancy word for behind.) Yes, love has meaning and value, but in this case, it doesn't pay the bills.

I'm not an expert, but here is some advice about money that will bring more comfort to the young than the old whose time may be running out. This is the advice I would give: Spend much less than you make. Have a disciplined saving and investment program and do that over a long period of time. Albert Einstein called compound interest the eighth wonder of the world! It would astound you how quickly you can build a nest egg. In Proverbs, Solomon declared, "The borrower is servant to the lender."

And speaking of the Bible, there's another character that had a lot of money and then lost everything he owned. His name was Job, and he got all of what he lost back, just like you can with the help of the Peanut Butter Promise. We hope you acquire a lot of it through integrous ways. Spend some, save some, and give some—no wait, give a whole bunch, and we'll pray you have plenty of it.

## 5. Career

While giving a plant tour to a few of his suppliers that he had known for years while working at Mercury Racing, where my brother Dale worked, he was asked this question.

"How many people work here?"

"About half," he answered jokingly.

The topic of career or service is not complicated. It deals with the workplace, or for those fortunate souls like Dale who once had cushy corporate jobs and retired, this could mean an area of service. I'm just kidding. My brother is nothing but a blessing, and today, he serves his family beautifully and unselfishly. If you're retired, we say congratulations. If you're looking for places to serve, ask your friends, pastor, and others. There's always room for another couple of hands at the food pantry or thrift store.

If you're still working, it is imperative that while you are pursuing your purpose—that arena where you want to make your mark, but most importantly, make a living—it's imperative to have a DreamGoal to land in your area of expertise. If you're still battling in this area, feel free to go back to the section "7 Powers of the Peanut Butter Promise" to review what we discussed there—your calling, that is—what you should be doing for your work, career, your vocation. It will be something you enjoy doing. If it requires patience, you'll have patience; if it requires you to handle the rigors of travel, you'll be able to do that.

Here's hoping that you find, as Michael W. Smith used to sing, your "Place in This World." If you can, you'll be working at the right place, and if you're retired, you'll be able to serve others like my brother Dale.

## 6. Health

Many times, we think of health as our physical health, but that's just the start. There is also mental and spiritual health, but for some of us, maybe the most important is our emotional health. With this in mind, in the spirit of The Principle of Responsibility, I look in the mirror and I find the enemy—the one armed with potentially toxic emotions—and the enemy is me!

The area of personal health, for the purpose and explanation of this philosophy, will encompass all of those emotions. The discussion about the deep relationship between our physical life and our emotions, and vice versa, can be complicated.

Any blessings that come from the fulfillment of our purpose through the Peanut Butter Promise may be found in recognizing a few things about our environment. Physical challenges can lead to emotional issues, and emotional issues can lead to physical issues. What is important for me, and possibly you, is that we take an honest inventory of where we are in these two areas. If you have to make adjustments, take a deep breath and go under and do it.

Trust me, I know all about mental, spiritual, physical, and emotional pain. When I found myself at the bottom in 1991, I was a mental, physical, spiritual, and emotional wreck. What came first was a flood of emotions from my many poor choices that led to the alcohol, sugar, and food in excess—or was it my aches and pains in my body that caused the anxiety and depression? Only God knows, but what was important for me was, as we indicated in The Principle of Responsibility, we must totally own up to where we are and what we are doing.

Let's discuss the opinions of the physical realm. My life has certainly shown there are three aspects that are instrumental for my overall health. They are exercise, diet/nutrition, and rest. Their priority is different for everyone. There was a time I felt that exercise was the best for me. Then, I came to the conclusion that a poor diet would doom any physical activity. And after a lot of fatigue, I came to the conclusion, and really only in the past few years, that rest is the most vital to attain my personal Peanut Butter Promise peak performance. It's a total package deal. Get to know thyself and your proclivities in every realm.

Be your own best friend and deal with your emotions, or they will deal with you. During his weekly *Your Move* television show, Andy Stanley shared this sobering statement made by Amanda Palmer that he heard on *The Tim Ferris Show*. It's in regard to the importance of dealing with issues. Palmer says, "If you don't deal with your demons, they go into the cellar of your soul and lift weights."

Wow. I don't know about you, but I would call that statement incredibly denial-busting. I can attest that until I had a serious talk with the man in the mirror and chose to work on my stuff, my demons looked like Arnold Schwarzenegger. I think I have given myself enough to work on in this area.

I've come to learn that so many of my circumstances, situations, or moods are really a symptom of something deeper going on. With that in mind, I need to dig into a problem and rip it out by the roots. There was a man who was constantly wiping away cobwebs with a broom. A curious man watching him eventually asked, "What are you doing?"

"I'm cleaning away a spider web," the man remarked.

"Yeah, I see that, but maybe it would be better if you killed the spider."

Many of my issues, especially those that involve my emotions, require me to get to the root of the issue. If I don't, I'll be continuing to swat at the webs when what I really need to do is kill the spider.

## 7. Personal

One of the things we like to do is play a fun game of Crazy Eights. Mom, Charlene, my brother Dan, and Cousin Patty will deal hands for hours on end, laughing and joking most of the time. The jokes are funnier when I'm winning, but that is for another time and another lesson. I can be a bit competitive, OK?

That is a personal activity that we like to do. Feel free now to dream about some things on your bucket list that may not be as important as others but are things that wouldn't violate your Peanut Butter Promise as you achieved them. How about a trip to Hawaii? That's one that is on our list. Maybe we can do one of our live events there? How about a trip to watch your favorite sports team play? You know, one thing I've never done and would like to do is watch a professional tennis tournament. My doctor suggested watching a golf tournament, but I told him that sport is too slow. I need more exercise than that.

Although it may sound a bit brash, how about setting a personal DreamGoal to get your estate in order? It's not pleasant to talk about, but extra credit goes to Peanut Butter Promise Players who have an estate plan, write their obituary, and plan their funeral. Of the many lessons from my dad, this one was one of the toughest but most valuable.

Yes, death is not always fun to talk about, but can we suggest that if you have not already done it, take care of some of these details. Having to make decisions on cemetery plots and funeral arrangements while in the depths of grief is devastating to those left behind. Plan as much as you can beforehand so family does not have to make these last-minute decisions, freeing them to grieve.

And remember you can't take it with you. If you could, there would be IRS people at the cemetery! I'm just trying to lighten things up a bit. But the truth is we would be most wise to spend a good share of time preparing for death, which is inevitable. One of the many lessons Pop taught was that all roads lead to Empire, which is our family cemetery.

That completes the seven DreamGoal categories of the Peanut Butter Promise. We're certainly not saying those are the only seven.

Below is an illustration showing what we call the Gears of Life of the Peanut Butter Promise. You'll note the seven DreamGoal categories in the middle and how the other content we've discussed up until now surrounds it. Let us be clear that the program you have just read is one we have come up with over the past twenty-five years. There are others. We're not going to tell you it is the best one. Just like me, it is a work in progress. Feel free to "eat the meat and spit out the bones."

Now, we present the Gears of Life of the Peanut Butter Promise, which is followed by four steps you may use to determine what DreamGoals to achieve and how to achieve them. We would like to reemphasize here that the gears, and the information encompassed in them, serve as only suggestions; there is no right or wrong to do any of this, unless what you are doing lacks integrity.

# The Gears of Life of The Peanut Butter Promise

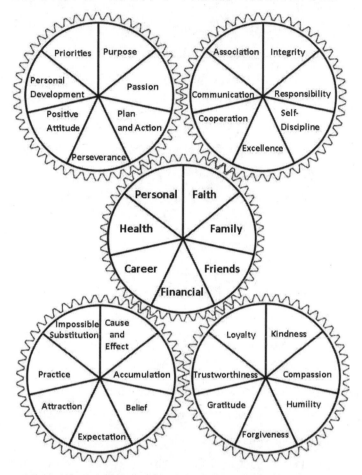

At the center of our life can be the 7 Categories of The Peanut Butter Promise. They are surrounded by The 7 Powers of The Peanut Butter Promise (top left); The 7 Principles of The Peanut Butter Promise (top right); The 7 Laws of The Peanut Butter Promise (bottom left); and The 7 Virtues of The Peanut Butter Promise (bottom right). Together, these 5 gears mesh, allowing us to fulfill our God-given purpose.

Now, it's *your* program, but the Peanut Butter Promise highly suggests you have a DreamGoal in each of the seven categories. And now, we get into the heart and guts of the program. Here is a copy of a DreamGoal Achievement Sheet and a few steps of the DreamGoal-setting process.

**Make a Wish List.** This involves filling out the top portion of the Wish List. This is where you list everything you would like to have and, more importantly, become. Charlene and I have come to learn there are good ideas and "God" ideas, and it's much better to pursue the latter. Wishes do not become DreamGoals until they are turned into them, and in this philosophy, you do that by filtering them through the next valuable step.

**Put the wishes to the test.** Refer to the three questions at the bottom of the DreamGoal Wish List. This philosophy suggests this process is best achieved through a written plan. These questions pretty much cut to the chase about your motives and your intentions, which are the who, what, and why. Once each Wish has passed the test, advance to the next step.

**Complete a DreamGoal sheet.** Once the DreamGoal has passed the test, put it to action and begin. Why is this so important? Well, let's just say there was once a good idea you had. You let it go too long, and it passed. Now, this probably has not happened to you, but let's just say it has. What happens is the idea loses its luster, its glow; the very vision can pass and go to the next Peanut Butter Promise Player who will act on it.

Jim Rohn called this fading of our Wish as the Law of Diminishing Intent. Have you ever heard the phrase "Use it or lose it?" Maybe that's a stretch, but I think you get the drift. It's brutal, but for some of your Wishes, it can be now or never for many reasons. I assure you that you have very little to lose if you set a DreamGoal and plenty to lose if you do not.

**Take action immediately.** Charlene and I try to review our most important DreamGoals monthly and the ones that deserve attention more often, especially if they are new. The ability to adhere to this practice will show your commitment, or lack thereof, to the DreamGoal. There is one very important aspect to this part of the program: It is not only normal but, many times, imperative to adjust the DreamGoal. Maybe it's too big or too small. Maybe the deadline should be put out a bit, maybe moved up. Feel free to rip up any sheet and start over. It happens here all the time. The Peanut Butter Promise comes to fruition more often than not for those who inspect what they expect.

**Proceed until the DreamGoal is achieved.*** Once you begin to take action, keep going until the DreamGoal is achieved. *That said, there are cases where it is necessary to suspend or completely halt certain DreamGoals. This may be when you see a lack of progress, or it is clear you should not continue with the pursuit of the DreamGoal any longer. And may we suggest you pray unceasingly for your DreamGoals and invite others to do the same for you?

**Example**

# The Peanut Butter Promise DreamGoal Program
# DreamGoal Wish List

| Category | The DreamGoal Wish |
|----------|--------------------|
| **Faith –** | I/We will attend worship services regularly. |
| **Family –** | I treat Charlene and my family with respect. |
| **Friends –** | I/We will seek, find, and keep good and faithful friends. |
| **Financial –** | I/We will seek to retire with $777,000 in an investment account. |
| **Career –** | I/We will seek to own our own bottle-washing business. |
| **Health –** | I/We will exercise at least four times per week. |
| **Personal –** | I/We would like to go to Hawaii for our seventeenth wedding anniversary! |

| DreamGoal Test Questions |
|--------------------------|

Is this DreamGoal congruent with my/our purpose?     Yes   No

Is this DreamGoal realistic based on my/our situation?     Yes   No

Is this DreamGoal good for everyone involved?     Yes   No

If the answer to these important questions for your DreamGoal
is not a bold YES, then discard it immediately. If it has passed
the test, then proceed to set a written DreamGoal ASAP.

## Example
# The Peanut Butter Promise DreamGoal Program
# The DreamGoal Sheet

| The DreamGoal is: |
|---|
| I will work at the Acme Company as an accountant. |

| The Plan and Action |
|---|

- I will professionally put together a competent resume and send it to Joe Johnson at Acme.

- I will exchange my services of forty hours per week at Acme Company for $37.07 per hour.

- After I have this position, I will daily read at least one hour of educational content in this area.

- I will attend at least two seminars per year. I will ask Acme Company to pay for this training.

- I will seek a relationship with Bob Jones, who will help me become a better accountant.

- During this time, I will do my best and give my all, as I feel this DreamGoal agrees with my purpose.

**DreamGoal start date: 12/25/2020**     **DreamGoal completion date: 12/25/2021**

Signed _____, _____/_____/20 _____

The DreamGoal Achievement Program has served me well since 1994, specifically through filling out and executing DreamGoal sheets. I think one of the benefits of these written prayer petitions is they allow us to, as Stephen Covey says in *The 7 Habits of Highly Effective People*, "Start with the end in mind." And one of the many keys is to allow your Peanut Butter Promise Partners to help you; after all, that's what they are there for.

I want to share with you the first DreamGoal I set and achieved through this system. This initial success convinced me that the system has merit, and thus, I've used it for over twenty-five years. It was August 10, 1994; I shuddered when I stepped onto the scales, but truth is good—I was 194 pounds. That moment was necessary for me to wake up and realize I needed to make a change. So, in a notebook, I wrote the facts and the plan to go from 194 pounds to 169 pounds. I'd start on the date above and complete the DreamGoal by October 12, 1994, which was a period a bit longer than seven weeks.

As I write this, I have the tattered notebook nearby. I can tell you that I did get to 169 pounds by October 12, but actually, I was at 167 pounds a few days before! But just to make things right, I put those two pounds back on! Yes, that's strange that I would do that, but not the strangest thing I've ever done, for sure.

DreamGoals are very important; they serve as targets for us. For a time at "The Rose Home of Rest, Relaxation, and Laughter," inhabited for a time by Pop, Mom, Charlene, and me, one of the activities was Pop's Banana Peel Toss. This consisted of Pop standing about seven feet away from the garbage basket, which was the target. For a few weeks, he'd just lob and drop them in the basket. But one day, I took a big brown envelope and drew a bullseye target and taped it onto the wall above the basket. That gave my father something to aim at.

DreamGoals are good targets, but as we set them, we must remember to "stay in our lane," which is not to do things others should be doing. Years ago my Pop learned this the hard way about not "staying in his lane," when he learned he wasn't a dentist. Late one night, about 11 p.m., Mom saw Dad in the kitchen with pliers in his hand, pointing them toward his mouth.

"What are you going to do?" she asked.

"I'm going to pull my tooth," he informed her.

"Not in here you aren't."

So, he decided to take the location of his self-appointed oral surgery to his office in the barn. With tool in hand, he yanked and cranked on his tooth, and suddenly, the tooth broke in half! Still in pain, he decided to call his dentist, which may have been the thing to do in the first place—maybe? Fortunately for my father, the dentist instructed him to come to his office, which was about a twenty-minute drive away. I'm sure for Pop it seemed much longer on that occasion.

Finally, Dad was in the dentist chair, and after a few minutes of poking with those sharp and annoying tools they use, he paused, stepped in front of my dad, and gave him his diagnosis and treatment plan.

"David, based on the injury created, the swelling, and the tooth being so close to a nerve to the brain, I'm going to just give you some medicine to take and have you come back in a few days."

"What?" my father retorted. "No, I'm not leaving till you pull my tooth."

There was a stare down that lasted a few seconds, but finally, the dentist relented with strong caution.

"David, you need to know that if we pull your tooth because of the situation, you could get brain damage."

Pop looked at him and said, "Well, it's midnight. I tried to pull my own tooth, so it seems that maybe I already have brain damage."

From then on, he left dental work to the dentist and stuck to tasks and DreamGoals that were in line with his purpose, and we can take a lesson from that. Thank goodness, the Peanut Butter Promise is not like pulling teeth.

The DreamGoal Achievement Program will work for you, and if you need any help, as always, we're here to help.

That's a Peanut Butter Promise.

# 7 SEEDS OF SERVICE OF THE PEANUT BUTTER PROMISE

### BY CHARLENE ROSE

**M**any years ago, an innocent little girl sat next to her sweet-scented and very loving grandmother, who had her arms around her. The little girl looked up at her and said, "Grandma, when you get old, I'm gonna take care of you!"

Her grandmother's response made the little girl wonder.

"Oh, child!" Grandma laughed. "You are so sweet!" to which the young child responded, "I'm gonna, Grandma! You'll see!"

Almost twenty years later, a young mother had just finished getting her sons onto the school bus when she had a thought enter her mind: "It's time!" She walked back into the old country farmhouse and sat down at her dark oak dining room table to read her morning devotions. She then went into her living room and sat down on the seafoam green antique couch she had gotten from her grandma a while back.

She gazed out the picture window at the beautiful blue sky while listening to the birds singing in the trees. Focusing on the branches that swayed in the wind, she uttered a prayer.

"Lord, what is it time for?"

She stood up and was thanking God for all he had given her when she looked at the couch. "Grandma!" she exclaimed.

Her thoughts went back to the time as a little girl when she made the promise to take care of her. She knew right away what had to be done. She called her grandmother.

She reminded Grandma of her conversation when she was a young girl. To her surprise, her grandmother remembered. She told her it was time, and her grandmother agreed and shared that she was just sitting there thinking about how she could continue to live in her own home and not be a burden to her family. Her grandmother asked her and her family to come live with her in the duplex (apartment) next to her. She said she would be able to stay in her home then.

"I'll talk to my children and let you know!" Grandma said.

"Grandma, before I hang up, there is something I need to ask you. Why did you laugh when I told you as a little girl I would take care of you when you were older?"

She began to laugh again and said, "I was already in my seventies back then!"

Both she and her grandma were laughing now because Grandma was ninety years old!

I'd like to share with you now my "7 Seeds of Service of the Peanut Butter Promise." Before I do, I'd like to share with you through the lady who influenced my life with them, my grandma.

They are: **Love**, **Attitude**, **Sacrifice**, **Humility**, **Wisdom**, **Patience**, and **Meet-the-Need**. Let's get started.

## 1. Love

The time I spent living with my grandmother was so very special. Over the last three years of her life, I was able to share many treasured moments with her. As I was there to help her stay in her home, she was there to help the Lord show me the true meaning of unconditional love. No condition!

You now know that the little girl in the story is me, and it's true. I still remember the days we shared those memories. God has been there with me through all of my days, and is in control of my past and its memories, the present, and the future. He is my source of truth and guides me in all of these memories. It was His love that Grandma shared with me during these years, and I finally realize it.

When my grandma and I began to spend our days together, we talked about many things. We laughed when she shared stories about earlier days. There was one in particular that involved her younger and very mischievous brother Harry. He always pranked his sister throughout his life. After Grandma married, Harry dressed up like a, well, let's just say a "lady of the evening," with high heels, a wig, dress, and all. Harry knocked on her door.

"Is your husband home?" he asked. "I'm looking for my wild man." In a high-pitched tone, he called out his name.

Grandma couldn't see her brother's face because he had it covered and had disguised his voice. She was becoming upset when he began to laugh. When she realized it was Harry, it was something they would always talk and laugh about when they came together. Oh, how she loved him.

When she was a young girl in the second grade, her life took a turn. Her mother and father removed her from school to help them in the family-owned store. She also had to help care for her baby brother Harry. She never complained or even regretted that she cared for him. She did all that was expected of her out of obedience because she loved her parents. No matter what, she knew she should never disrespect or talk back to them.

From eight years old into adulthood, Grandma worked full time. If not in the store, it was at home with Harry and her grandmother. She loved her grandmother as well and would learn so much from her about how to take care of the home, gardening, baking, and so on. She loved spending time with her grandmother.

Always thinking of how she could help out, she gave her best work doing the most she could. Whether it was scrubbing floors, changing a diaper, or weeding the garden, she never complained. It was hard, but she wouldn't have traded the experience and memories she gained through it. She loved her family so much.

Grandma told me she had faith in God because, as a young girl, her family attended church every Sunday, and she loved to go there. Just before she was taken out of school at eight years old, she said she was walking home and thought she heard someone tell her He loved her and would always be there with her and would help her through her life.

She said she knew it was God but didn't know why she knew it. She said something happened that day. She felt good inside, and she was not afraid.

So, every day, she would talk to Him and read devotions that helped her focus on good things. Whenever she cooked or cleaned or even planted her garden, she would always be thinking of others and how she could bless them.

I would help her plant a garden or do Christmas baking with her. She would always have boxes she saved for when we completed the harvest or made the treats. She'd tell me to line each box with foil and put some of each vegetable or a variety of cookies (at Christmastime) in each one. I'd decorate each box.

She would send me down the street to the widower and his son and hand them a box. Next, I would go to the divorced lady with the five children who lived on the corner. Then, I'd take a box to the lady across the street.

Grandma even sent a large box to the neighbor who lived next door, who had a special needs son and a sickly husband. The neighbor was not always an easy-to-get-along-with person toward others, including my grandma.

I asked my grandma a question. "Why do you give her the biggest box, especially with the way she treats you?'

It was then she said this and taught me something I'll never forget.

"Honey, it's always better to give than to receive."

Grandma didn't do it so the lady would be her friend or be kind to her. She expected nothing in return. She did it because she cared about the family. She saw their need for love, not judgment. She did it because she loved her neighbor, even though her neighbor didn't love her back. Grandma did this for all of them until she died. She taught me to "Love your neighbor as yourself!" Grandma knew God loved her through Jesus Christ, so she did what she learned from Jesus.

Grandma wasn't the richest monetarily, but she would do everything for others in love because it was a free gift she could give away, and the greatest of these is love. In love, she went above and beyond the need. By the way, her family also received this same love from her. We knew she loved us.

## 2. Attitude

One special Christmas, Grandma had us all over for a meal. We were dressed in our new clothes we got for the occasion. She had a new coloring book and crayons for each one of her younger grandchildren to color while we waited for dinner. She had decorated her home so beautifully with brightly colored lights draped around a silver Christmas tree adorning the big picture window.

On that day, she served us a huge dinner of freshly baked ham and rolls, mashed potatoes, gravy, cranberries, salads, and homemade pies, using her best china and crystal dishes. We knew she spent days getting prepared for it. There was music and laughter as adults shared stories about their younger days and the children ate the treats and candy she gave us. Those were such good memories for all of us children; it was a very special time.

Did I mention that Grandma was in her seventies and suffering from rheumatoid arthritis, or that her husband was sickly and had need of her care daily as well? Grandma was amazing.

She would wake up early every morning, bathe herself, dress, and make a breakfast of oatmeal, take care of grandpa, then prepare for the coming celebration. She would spend hours and hours on one meal for a very large family gathering. She never complained about any of it. She had an attitude of thanksgiving. It was always enjoyable helping her prepare throughout the week before; we talked about good times from days past and would share so many family stories.

She pulled out the family albums of pictures from past celebrations, picnics in the park, birthdays, and so on for us to enjoy. We loved being around her. She was always smiling and made us feel loved. Her home was always filled with peace, no matter what was happening.

Shortly after Grandpa died, Grandma was sitting in a wicker chair outside on her front porch when she overheard a family member share something about her that was not true and was very misleading. It was an awful hurt to her heart. Because the person didn't know she could hear them, she decided to forgive that person. She realized that what they said would be something they would have to live with. She treated the person as if she had never wronged her. She decided to stay kind even when someone else chose to hurt her. What an incredible choice.

## 3. Sacrifice

As Grandma would share her life experiences with me, I realized she had sacrificed so much throughout her years. As a young eight-year-old, her parents decided to take her out of school. I'm sure she would have liked to stay in school and learn more or play with other children, but that was not to be. It was the end of learning anymore about reading, writing, and arithmetic (math) in school. A second-grade education was all Grandma would have, but the wisdom she learned and passed on came from something a textbook could never teach.

This young girl took care of her family at home by helping with the cooking, cleaning, laundry (with a wringer washer and hanging clothes outside on the line), gardening, and taking care of her little brother and, later, her grandmother as well. At the store, she helped stock shelves and take care of customers' needs, measured flour and sugar, and so on. I think you get the point. She said she learned enough arithmetic to help her mother with bookkeeping at the store.

Grandma learned measurements from her mother and grandmother when they taught her to cook and sew. Remember, she started at eight years old. She also shared details of her mother's disappointment in her and the high expectations she had toward her, which made it very difficult for her to keep her mind on the good things. For some reason, she just knew her mother worked very hard as well and that life wasn't easy for her either. So she persevered through the years without much time to be a child.

When she became an adult, Grandma was a servant. She had learned so much by helping her parents and her grandmother that she became a good cook and was able to take care of people who were ill, injured, or in need. Her grandmother taught her what to use and how to treat all kinds of sicknesses and injuries. She would use this knowledge throughout her adult life for family, friends, and neighbors.

Because she had to stop going to school at a young age, she was never able to go back, and that was hard for her to cope with. She also did not have any close friends because of the demands put on her at home and at the store. Grandma was never able to go to football games, school dances, or participate in other activities. She never learned how to drive a car. Believe me, she would have liked to. Yet she pressed on, being grateful for what she had.

## 4. Humility

Grandma's mother became ill, and after her father died, Grandma took care of her. She recalled her mother still having a hardened heart toward her. Even so, she moved her mother into her home, all while trying to raise her two children. Her mother would say and do things that were unkind to her when she would take care of her.

Through her tears, Grandma shared something with me.

"Charlene, I never understood why Mother didn't like me."

Even so, Grandma still told her mother how much she loved her and thanked her for the things she taught her. With tear-filled eyes, she told me her mother never told her she loved her, but she said, "I believed she did."

Grandma was always good to all of us, no matter what we were like. When my grandpa was becoming ill, he lost his balance easily. He was driving his car, and some people were on the porch watching him as he drove up to the house. He drove up the curb on his way into the driveway. As Grandma was standing there, they were all laughing and making fun of his driving. Grandma said her heart sank as she listened to their abusive comments.

That day turned out to be the last day Grandpa drove. She quietly went down the stairs and, without saying a word, met Grandpa and helped him into the house. That's humility. Grandpa was never the same from that day on. As it turned out, he needed brain surgery, and after that, Grandma gave good and loving care to him until his death.

## 5. Wisdom

In the song I wrote for my grandma, there is a phrase in the chorus that says, "It's your wisdom I depend upon. It's giving me strength and helping me to carry on." One of the greatest gifts God gave Grandma was wisdom. She had the ability to make good choices and decisions by using it. As you can see, the things I am writing about contain so much of her wisdom because she shared it in the way she talked. All that she did displayed the vast wisdom she attained from her many life experiences.

Grandma decided to put a small apartment in her home. She didn't need to live in her big house alone, and the unit she was preparing would have access to the upstairs part of the home because she was no longer able to climb those steps. She hired a carpenter to build a set of stairs in the back of the house to connect the upstairs to the new apartment. He was working on the bottom few stairs and was sitting in her back hall when she noticed the man was perplexed.

"Why do you look so confused?" she asked.

"Well, the steps now meet the back hallway, but I'm not sure where to take the stairway from here."

She looked at what he did and said, "That's an easy fix."

Grandma then proceeded to tell him to make a platform where he stopped. To the right was the entrance to the apartment, so she suggested he put three steps leading into the apartment. To his left was the entrance to the back hallway, so she told him to put two steps that way to reach the platform that led to the outside stairs.

He looked at her and said, "In all of my years of carpentry, I have never had anyone have to show me what to do. I've been sitting here for a while and could not for the life of me figure this out. And an older lady comes and looks at it and, in seconds, tells me how to fix my dilemma."

He also said, "Maybe it's time for me to retire."

Grandma and I laughed about this. The man asked how she figured it out so easily. She said she could see it in her mind and she had done similar remodels in her last home to separate it into apartments.

Through laughter, she looked at me and said, "This little four-foot-ten, gray-haired widow with a second-grade education shows up and tells this man how to do his job that he specialized in and took away any ego he may have had."

Many talks with Grandma over the years have given me an ability to work through many hardships, past failures, and experiences. She would share things with me and would have no idea, at that time, I'd been praying for God to show me what to do about certain situations. It was as if she knew what was in my heart. She shared experiences with me about her life that I needed to hear at just the right time as well. She was such a gift from God to me, and I will always treasure every memory of her. When I read about wisdom in my Bible, there are a few places where I would write her name next to certain verses. She is far above rubies. Now, I'm sharing her wisdom with you!

## 6. Patience

When it came to patience, Grandma had that down. She didn't fumble on it with me when I would arrive later than I thought to help her do her cleaning because I'd been finishing chores at my home. She was always gracious when I'd tell her I was going to be a bit late. If that was going to be the case, she just wanted to know. She was a very patient person.

One of the times I saw her practice a lot of patience was when she had a man (whom she loved like a son), who would come over once a month for a few days to do yardwork, painting, and repairs at her house. He worked for her for many years. This one particular time, he hadn't showed up, and she tried calling him. He didn't answer and she was concerned that something might have happened to him.

You see, this man was an alcoholic. Sometimes he would drink for days and lose track of time. At times, he wouldn't even know what day it was. So when he didn't show up to work, Grandma would pray for him while sitting in her black recliner, waiting for him to come.

On one occasion, he showed up a few days late. When he did show up, he was sober and stayed that way until all of the work for Grandma was completed.

She had him come inside with her before he started to work. She had him pull up a chair right in front of hers as she listened to him share the truth of what happened. He never lied to her. He gave all the details of the sadness he faced that caused him to drink excessively.

At that moment, Grandma pointed her crippled forefinger at him and spoke to him quietly.

"I'm disappointed in you. You gave me your word that you would be here on Monday."

"I'm so sorry," he said.

With moistened eyes, he lowered his head. She took his hand in hers, and with tears flowing from her own eyes, she said to him, "When I couldn't reach you, I was very concerned. I love you like a son. Nothing will ever change that. I forgive you. Now, let's get some work done!"

He took the list and went outside and started working.

## 7. Meet-the-Need

Well, as you can probably see, my grandma was a very special lady, one of a kind. Grandma's daughter would come by during the week to take care of her shopping and laundry. She also spent time assisting Grandma with her bills and banking. Because Grandma really only needed my help on Wednesdays and evenings, I was able to work a part-time job at a health store.

The manager hired me right away because of my referral from a lady I had worked for since I was twelve. The person who hired me ignored the fact that I did not have a high school diploma or GED. I was only able to go to school through my tenth year. I thought that would be an issue at the time, but it wasn't. My manager taught me everything I needed to know to do a good job. I had to read books and learn about the products and what they were used for.

I watched her very closely as to how she did things, and I did my best to do the same. She was good with the customers, but I could tell after we had a remodel of the store that she was getting tired, so one day, she came to me with an opportunity.

"How would you like my job?"

I was confused, so I asked her a question.

"What is it that you know about me that I don't?"

"Well, I know you can do the job," she said.

She went on to tell me she would train and show me what I needed to know before she left. I asked my family and Grandma what they thought about the offer. They all said I should give it a try. So, I told my manager yes, and as soon as I did, she quit before I could be trained properly.

The senior store manager was unable to train me, so I trained myself. At that moment, I was determined to make it through. I promised myself I would do things differently for all of my employees. On my own, I had to figure out how to do the weekly paperwork that needed to be completed after closing out the cash register every Thursday. I went into the files from previous weeks and did the best I could by following the example. Well, I did OK. (I do not recommend this for anyone!) I also called a manager from another store who became a very good friend to me. She walked me through a few things, including ordering the products and the quantity.

One time, during an annual store inventory, the lady from the home office told me I had errors in just one area of my paperwork.

She asked, "Who showed you how to do your weekly report?"

I explained my situation to her, and she was totally impressed. My store was in good shape and so were our sales. We had received a "Best Store" award that year.

What I loved about the job the most was serving the people, employees, and customers alike. A customer would come into the store, and we had a rule that you had five seconds to acknowledge them when they came in. You never asked them *if* you could help them. You asked *how* you could help them. Meeting the customer's needs was why we were there.

I had only one employee who worked with me after the manager quit, so I had to hire and train two new employees. I interviewed the candidates in my office and in the store. If there was a customer to attend to when they were with me, I would pay close attention to see how they listened and interacted with people. I looked for their interest in nutrition, but more importantly, their willingness to pick paper up off of the floor or straighten a product that was out of place on the shelves. Those were the ones I paid attention to. What was most important was that they cared about people and wanted to "Meet-the-Need." If they were willing to give great customer service, that was important.

The three employees I had were with me during the entire time I held my position as manager. I trained each of them to do the same things I had done. I was a part-time employee when I started, so I knew everything about their job. I would never ask them to do anything I had not already done myself. My position as manager meant I helped them do their job to the best of their ability. What I expected from them is what I did myself.

The store was like a child. I was training them on how to take care of and help me raise this child—in this case, the store. A good parent will not hand their baby to just anyone to care for it. They will find someone they can trust to do the job well. That person would be someone who would give the same care for them as if they were the parent.

I taught my employees to do things the way the company expected it to be done, but always make the customer their first priority. I trained them to realize that when they worked alone, I would either see their results from the sales or the well-stocked shelves and cleanliness of the store itself. It promoted excellence in their performance. They never sat around and did nothing. It was evident they were doing their job. They'd drop what they were doing and take the time to meet the needs of the customer as soon as they entered our store.

They were not to rush or hurry when dealing with them. They were to give them their complete and full attention. I taught them to do their best, to treat the customer as they would want to be treated.

I always did the same. I also told them to expect a customer to be someone who was watching the way they were doing their job and reporting it to the company. (Yes, there were secret shoppers for accountability that visited our store!)

I trained my employees about my job and included them when I did the paperwork and closed out the store for the week. When my Grandma died, I had three capable employees that ran the store without me for a week so I could take time to be with family and grieve. It went without a hitch; the store ran smoothly. While I was gone, sales were good, the store was stocked, and nothing needed immediate attention when I returned. It was as if I were there the whole time.

When I had my third child, I decided to quit so I could raise her. I asked one employee if he wanted my position. He was shocked that I asked him, and to that, I could relate, but I shared with him that I was confident in his abilities.

"I've taught you everything you need to know to do this job," I said. "You are capable of running this store. You also have two very competent, well-trained employees to help you."

He was very nervous at the thought of managing the store, but I assured him I would be right here for him until he was ready, and I would not leave before that.

After he agreed to take my place, I gave a one-month notice to my boss and let my employee do my job for two weeks as I oversaw his work. When I completed the last day of work, I assured him he was ready and made a promise.

"If you have any questions, I am only a phone call away."

He called me only once. He managed the store for over a year and was promoted to a store in Chicago, where he was training for a district manager position. One day, I received a letter from him. In it, he thanked me for believing in him and training him like I did. He went on to do very well.

Because of the not-so-comfortable position I was placed in to be manager, I decided to teach my employees a better way, and it was accomplished. We must be willing to put others' needs ahead of our own, doing our best to meet them, and our needs will be met.

Guess where I learned that from? Grandma! She told me something when I was taking care of her needs one day. She said I should take care of others when they have need because when I am older, I will have someone to take care of me. Just like her!

As you may have noticed, throughout this chapter, all of the seven seeds of the Peanut Butter Promise are planted together in the same garden. That is because you can't have one without the other. To be like Grandma is to be a person of excellence. (I didn't say perfect!) This represents the fruit of the seven seeds. What I learned is to go beyond the call of duty. If asked to go one mile, go two. Go the distance. Trust the timing and be on time. When you know what to do and when to do it, do it with all your might. And keep growing. Be your best you.

Where are you getting your nourishment or fertilization from? What are you reading, or who are you listening to or spending most of your time with? Ask questions of those who are where you want to be. Hang out with like-minded people who value your gifts, and be sure to value theirs. Give away the fruit of your labor to those who need it. Believe me, it will return to you someday.

My grandma was my best friend. She taught me how to love, give, serve and, most importantly, forgive. I hope you will read this chapter more than once. Allow it to do for you what these moments with Grandma did for me.

# CONCLUSION

# KEEPING OUR PEANUT BUTTER PROMISE

Charlene and I were stunned. We'd just got off the phone with Dr. Atassi. The crux of our concern was that, barring a miracle, at fifty-seven years young, Charlene would soon be caring for two in diapers. Oh no, not in *that* way, but it seemed inevitable she'd be taking care of two in that way soon—and one would be me. Although aspects of the Peanut Butter Promise help bring predictability into our life, our circumstances we face… not so much.

A biopsy had revealed I had cancer, and it needed attention sooner rather than later. Still numb, a few hours later, we were sitting with Dr. Omar Atassi, who is one of the finest people and communicators we've ever known. He was giving Charlene and me our treatment options. After much prayer, we chose surgery to remove my prostate. And sure enough, in a few months, Charlene did indeed have two in diapers. Stay tuned.

There are times in our lives that are pivotal, that have the potential to propel us toward our purpose or pull us away from it. Charlene and I landed in the epicenter of the Peanut Butter Promise on March 24, 2018. It was a warm, pleasant spring day in our parts. A slew of our family had just sat down for a bite to eat after visiting our father in the hospital. He was ninety years young in the spirit of his heart, but his physical heart was failing. Sitting at a table with us was my sister Gloria, my brother-in-love Randy, my brother Jim straight across from us, and my brother Dan to our right.

We were also discussing our mother Jean who was eighty-seven at the time. Just the summer before, in July of 2017, Charlene could see that Mom wasn't feeling well and immediately took her to the hospital, where the cardiologist said she needed a pacemaker, and one was subsequently inserted. A week later, Charlene noticed Mom was not getting any better, and she took her to the hospital, where we learned the current pacemaker was malfunctioning, so it was replaced immediately.

And only a few months later, in October, Charlene noticed that Mother was ashen-gray, out of breath, and weak. Because she had seen this before in someone else, she knew to immediately get Mom to the hospital, where it was determined that her lungs were filled with blood clots. Had she not gotten there, she very well would have been dead in a few hours. So, the meeting with my family was timely because, at the time, Charlene was constantly aware of Mom and Dad's health issues.

In the somewhat-distant past, it was not unusual for my family to not deal with issues that demanded attention and explanation. Not only was there an elephant in the room, but he was pooping all over the place. On this occasion of meeting, it was important to deal with another reality. The conversation involved recognizing that time had quickly taken its course and toll on our parents. We all came to the conclusion they needed more assistance than they had been getting from us *if* they were to be able to continue to stay in their home, which was always their plan.

Between bites, Dan looked at me and popped this question. "If we put a bed upstairs at Mom and Dad's, would you and Char be willing to move in to take care of them?" This request didn't come as a shock. Actually, Charlene had been telling me for the last three years that she could see very noticeably that both Mom and Dad were slipping. It was for that very reason my wife and I had increased our weekly visits from one to as many as three times a week to help them. Charlene would do dishes, dust, and the laundry, while I did light work of pushing a vacuum and strategically getting rid of some mail Dad was letting pile up.

Looking at Dan, I was somewhat relieved that, along with us, other family members, including his wife, Shirley, were becoming more and more aware that our parents were in need of help. Personally, I could never imagine Mom and Dad leaving their home and going into assisted living or another facility. Charlene and I were certainly the right choice for the task. Looking around the table that day, we saw that Gloria and Randy lived out of state, Jim had just retired and deserved to spend time with his family and grandchildren, and Dan still was plenty busy with work, family, and grandchildren. Not present were my brothers Gary and Dale, but at the time, they were also unable to fill the proposed full-time job.

Charlene and I were quite busy at the time of the proposal. We were about to embark on a tour to promote our highly rated national television documentary, *Only 16: Tragedy of 2 Billys*, which we'd filmed in 2017. Along with that, I was fixing to start writing this book. That said, the answer to the question came easy for us. I looked over at my wife; I could tell we were on the same page, and we both said, "Sure, we'll do it."

Dan, as if he knew our answer in advance, smiled and said to us, "Good. I brought the truck. We can go right from here to the mattress place and get you guys a bed." And when we finished eating, that's exactly what we did. Until a few years before, Mom and Dad were managing without family assistance. But Charlene had forewarned me earlier, "Things are going to be changing quickly for your folks, Steve. I've seen this before." I couldn't see it, but she was right. It's peculiar how the perils of Alzheimer's (Dad) and dementia (Mom) sneak in.

The decision to assist our parents was not difficult, especially for me, in that I couldn't live seven lives and pay them back for all they had meant and done for me. After all, the seven categories of the Peanut Butter Promise shows that family is right after faith, and what better way to exhibit faith than to take care of family.

So, it took forty-three years, but Dad's June of 1975 prophecy proclaiming that, "Someday I may end up moving back home with him and Mom" came true on March 26, 2018, the first night we stayed with them. What a joy—what an incredible journey it has been. It has been the absolute *best* decision Charlene and I have *ever* made, not only as a couple, but in each of our lives, and it landed us (as mentioned prior) in the epicenter of the Peanut Butter Promise, exactly where this book was written.

Dad was always an eternal optimist; he loved reading and learning all the way up till the end. He was a fearless patriot, a Packers fan, and made it known to everyone around him that we all had an obligation to take care of family, friends, our country, and to be grateful for every breath. One of his mantras was, "If you ain't having fun, you aren't doing it right."

Father was a fast mover whose passion for cattle was widely known. In the late '90s, he won an international award from SEMEX-Canada during the Royal Winter Fair. The award was in recognition for his dedication and lifetime support of Canadian livestock. He had been nominated by his boss and good friend Francis Costello who had made the trip with Dad and Mom to receive the award.

On the subject of cattle, our neighbor, Field Rahn (who is Dave and Donny's father) once said this about my father: "Dave Rose knows more about cattle than most people forget."

During our valuable time living with Pop, he told me, "Steve, I didn't learn to walk until I was fifty because up until then, I was running everywhere." I saw it. Many of his years in the 1960s and '70s were filled with him up at 5 a.m. for morning milking and chores, eating a quick breakfast, kissing mother, and going to artificially inseminate cows by day for East Central Breeders. He was usually home for milking and chores at night. He then read till eleven or so, hit the hay, and it repeated itself.

Mother's optimism is as equally infectious as Pop's. She's always found the best in every situation. She always has a song in her heart that can be heard coming from her mouth constantly. She raised the six of us, but really eight. I'll never forget the day I came home from school on May 3, 1967. I was lying on the bed with her when she said, "Go tell your brothers that your sister had twins today." I had no idea. As a matter of fact, I'd come to learn later that my brothers learned that fact on the school bus. The communication at the Rose home wasn't really good, but we found a way to put "fun" in dysfunctional. The family has come a long way since then but is still far from perfect. Needless to say, Mom was busy. Today, she loves to put puzzles together with Charlene. Maybe you've seen a few of them posted on Charlene's Facebook page.

Pop was an avid Cubs fan despite the fact their dugout was usually six feet deep by June. It was a glorious day in 2016 for him when the Cubbies finally won the World Series! We have Pop on video seconds after, professing, "The hundred-year rebuilding program is complete!" One of his lines about his favorite team was, "Any team can have a bad century."

Mom, who just turned ninety, is still quick-witted. When asked by her doctor if she wanted to be resuscitated if she died, she said, "No, once dead, always dead." A couple years ago on their anniversary, Dad asked Mom, "How long have you been married?" and she fired back "As long as you." One time, I asked Mom where she had gotten her gray hair, and she remarked, "From my kids." I don't think she was kidding. My favorite of her great quotes came the day she looked into Pop's eyes and said, "David, you look tired, you better go to church." Although Pop was the "head" of the family, make no mistake, Momma is the "heart" of it.

In retrospect, the possibility of Charlene and me moving in with my parents originated in 2015, just three years prior to the family meeting where Dan popped the question. Dad was at Froedtert Hospital being wheeled away for what many may call a "minor" heart procedure, a leaking aortic aneurism. Now, to me, "minor" heart surgery is the kind that someone *else's* father would be having, *not* mine. This was "major" surgery, a very serious procedure to us, and although Pop wasn't scared, I think he knew it would slow him down.

As he lay in one of those embarrassing gowns on the gurney-type bed, ready to head into surgery, the medical staff invited Mother to give Dad a kiss, and as they were rolling him away, he put his hand up to get the attention of the transporter.

"Excuse me. May I talk to my daughter-in-law (Charlene) a second?"

"OK," said the young man as he put Dad in reverse for about seven feet until he was looking up into her eyes.

"Char, will you do me a favor?"

"Of course, Pop, anything."

"If I make it through this surgery, will you help me be able to stay and die in my home?"

"You got it, Pop. I promise that I'll do everything I can to help you do that, OK?"

"Thank you, Char," he said, with blue eyes glistening as he was wheeled away. And with that, Charlene had made quite a profound Peanut Butter Promise, but the question was, would she be able to fulfill it? Stay tuned.

Dr. Rossi, one of the best in his trade, performed a successful surgery. Pop recovered, and life went on for both him and Mom. During the summer of 2018, Charlene noticed things happening with both Dad and Mom, but on this occasion, it was Father.

"Something's not quite right with Pop," she said.

"What do you mean?" I asked.

"He doesn't seem to be breathing right."

Without hesitation she declared, "I'm calling Doctor Patty."

On that note, she immediately grabbed her phone and called, and within a half hour, he was being checked out only a few miles from home. After a test, Dr. Patty pulled my wife aside.

"OK, his oxygen is way low, and it appears he is in congestive heart failure. I'm going to call an ambulance. He needs to get to the hospital for more tests." Within an hour, that is what was happening.

As per usual, my wife's hunch was right. Why the timing of this diagnosis was crucial was because Dad had been scheduled, within only a few days, to have another aortic aneurism heart procedure with Dr. Rossi. All this to say, the Lord works in mysterious ways; some pneumonia can be dealt with, other kinds are deadly, and because Charlene caught a few of Dad's symptoms, he was diagnosed and did not go into surgery. Only God knows for sure, but even Pop said later that he believed he probably wouldn't have come out of that surgery alive.

That would be the first of three times Charlene caught something that would have taken Dad out, and she takes none of the credit for it. The same for Mother, whose life was extended twice when Charlene noticed the symptoms of the heart issue and later blood clots.

Through all the adventures, a motivational wake-up for Pop went like this. I'd enter the bedroom and say, "Good morning, Dad! Today is (the day and date). The nurse and cook (Charlene) is waiting for you to check in. The Brewers play today at (time against whom)." And then, the most important info like, "Dad, (if applicable) you currently have a ten Banana Peel Toss streak, and to the best of my calculations, if you make your first two today, you will be back over .700!"

He'd then jokingly say something like, "Geez, Steve, that's pressure. People have no clue what this feels like." That's probably true—how many Banana Peel Toss players do you know of, especially those like Dad in the ninety-plus division? He was right in that there probably were not many banana peel tossers in the world, but I reminded him that it was all worth it.

"Yeah, I can't imagine, Pop," I would say. "But like a pitcher who is throwing a no-hitter, pressure is a privilege, right?"

He'd usually crack one more grin, lean his head slightly forward off of his pillow, lift both his legs about six inches from the mattress, and on a count of three, swing his slipper-laden feet and workout-panted legs over to the side of the bed, stand up, grab his glasses, and we were off to the races for another exciting day.

Having DreamGoals and a plan of action to fulfill them are powerful and necessary. The truth is some of the greatest DreamGoals we can be a part of helping to fulfill are those of others, and that's what we were in the process of doing for Mom and Pop. On Wednesday, August 7, 2019, Dad ambled into the kitchen, met us with his usual cheerful greeting, and hopped on the scales, which was part of the ritual. Charlene monitored and recorded the result in her notebook for Dr. Patty. Then, Pop sat down to take his customary three sets of his blood pressure. To make sure they were accurate, no red flags, he would then give them to my wife for review, which she did.

Charlene turned from where she was preparing Dad's breakfast bowl. The concoction was made of oatmeal, nuts, flax seed, blueberries, bananas, and chocolate protein. He turned his radio down from listening to Jay Weber on WISN radio and asked this question.

"Char, I have a question for you," he said as she set the bowl in front of him.

"Yes, Pop."

"Do you think I can make it to our seventieth wedding anniversary?"

That date was September 24, which was still almost seven weeks out.

Always one to weigh her words and having made a commitment to Dad that she would always be straightforward with him, she made the following prediction.

"Yes, I *do* think you can, Pop,"she said, adding this caveat, "but you're going to have to work with me."

A quick gaze at the calendar reminded us that this was somewhat bold, but doable. With this goal for Pop in mind, I decided to start a countdown on the calendar, the same one where we recorded Dad's daily Banana Peel Toss results.

And so, we started an official daily countdown in the left-hand corner of each day square on the calendar. Soon, it was back to school for the kids, the Major League baseball season was now in the late-summer pennant stretch, and it seemed like Pop (Mom, too) was going to be able to make it. And guess what? He and Mother did indeed make it to their seventieth wedding anniversary.

This proves one of the theories of the Peanut Butter Promise, which is this: It's important beyond measure to have DreamGoals. Look what this did for Father. He lived to celebrate Mother and his seventieth anniversary.

That day, after his breakfast, as usual, he stepped over to the Banana Peel Toss line, where he made his first throw, missed the next two, and then absolutely nailed the last two tosses, dead center. This gave him three out of five for the day, and best of all, his average remained over .700!

Then, he sat down and completed his normal routine, but Charlene noticed he was weaker than usual. After lunch, he began to quiver, and he mentioned that to her.

"Charlene, why am I shaking?"

"I don't know. Let's check your blood pressure, temperature, and oxygen," which she did before giving him a suggestion.

"I think you should go lay down, Pop."

Very slowly, and with Char holding his arm, he made it onto the bed, which is about twenty steps from the kitchen through the living room. Charlene made a call to Dr. Patty and reported her findings. The doctor instructed her to help Dad rest and, when he woke up, recheck his stats. If nothing changed, she was to call her back.

Dad slept the whole afternoon. He got up for supper, ate, and went back to lie down. My brothers came over. We had cake and ice cream as we sat around him. Mother was sitting on the bed with Pop as we each read our anniversary cards to them. Dad was grateful, but so exhausted. With closed eyes, he shared what had been a common theme over the last year.

"I'm so glad that I chose to marry your mother." Holding back tears, he said, "She did a wonderful job raising all of you."

Charlene then phoned the doctor on call, who said to bring Pop right in to the hospital. He didn't need an ambulance, but we should get him there soon. That stay was for three days. He came home on Saturday, September 28. We had Lawrence Welk cranked on the car stereo for the ride home. That afternoon was a beautiful fall day. Pop and Mom had a blast as Doug and Linda Hodorff, dear friends of the family, came over that afternoon. Doug busted out some cheese, Dad asked Charlene if he could have some beer with it, and she said of course. The pictures taken from that occasion are precious. That would turn out to be the last party—at least, the last one Pop would physically be here for.

On Monday, September 30, Pop was showing lots of fatigue and having more trouble breathing, so we took him back to the hospital. Charlene and I stayed with him in the emergency room. He was hooked up to all the usual lines that monitored his vitals. Charlene left to go to the bathroom and I sensed I should say something to Dad sooner rather than later.

I got up and leaned over to him. His eyes were closed, and I bucked up and made up my mind that I would not cry. It was hard as I shared this with him.

"Dad, in case I haven't told you lately, this last year-and-a-half has been the best time of my life, ever."

He said, "I agree, Steve."

I then sat down before I fell down. It was hitting me what was happening. I urge you, if you are ever in the same situation, to speak when you have the chance to. And what happened next really sucked. The doctor on duty drew the curtain so Dad could rest as the doctor approached us, sat down, and hit us right in the very middle of our guts.

"There are some things on his scan that have changed from when he was here last week." As you can imagine, he was quite apologetic. "I know I should be encouraging you," he said.

"It's OK. Please give it to us straight, Doctor. My father would want it no other way."

"Thank you," he practically whispered. "Your father has atypical pneumonia, which means that when he eats, he's aspirating, or getting food in his lungs. If he eats, he will die in due time. If he stops eating, well…"

"We understand," Charlene said, attempting to comfort him.

Well, here is the ironic part of this whole thing that revealed God's incredible sense of humor. For years, Dad's joke about eating was this: "I've heard that death by starvation is a terrible way to go. A lot of things may 'take me out,' but starvation won't be one of them."

This did give the doctor a bit of relief as we shared this with him. He then got up and told Dad what was happening, and Father confirmed, "No, I'm going to eat!" And with this, the doctor smiled and reached down to pat Dad's shoulder.

He then came over to us and said, "It is his time. If you would so choose, we can bring a hospital bed into his home. We will arrange for hospice to assist in the process. We will keep him overnight. We will release him tomorrow after we have the bed set up and the hospice staff ready to go." That was the beginning of the end, and now, we had to tell Pop. And just as Charlene has always said she would, she went over, grabbed Dad's hand, his eyes opened and met Charlene's, and she gave him the news.

"Pop, this is it. You are dying, and it won't be long. We're going to take you home as soon as everything is ready." She then explained that hospice would be coming into his home, that he would not be going to a hospice home. After reassuring him, he looked up at her and spoke.

"I wasn't expecting to go out this way, but I guess none of us ever really know."

It helped Charlene and me that he was very calm and had a peace, mainly because Charlene had reassured him he was going back home. In a few minutes, Dad was taken to a private room.

That next morning, Charlene and I went to go see Pop. Charlene tactfully left me alone with him. I sat next to Father on one of those round chairs with wheels and no backing. I held his hand as we talked about the fun we had together, especially the last year-and-a-half.

As he laid there with his eyes closed and a peaceful smile on his face, he posed a really good question to me—a really good one.

"Steve."

"Yes, Pop."

"Have you ever thought about what will live on through you, in others, when you're gone?"

I'm never one to be lost for words, but that question gave me great pause.

"Wow, that's a great question, Pop."

And then what he said next blessed me beyond measure.

"I think I'll live through you, Steve."

I smiled and said, "Dad, you've been living through me most of my life. Who do you think gave me the bug for personal growth and development? That was you. Ever since you took me to the PMA rally in 1977 where I heard Zig Ziglar and the others, I've wanted to be a public speaker for twenty-five years. Your name has come up in everything Charlene and I have done over the last few years, and it always will."

The rest of our conversation dealt with how he wanted Charlene and me to stay with and take care of Mother and a few other things regarding the family. I thank the Lord for that quiet alone time with my father that day. I've known many who never got that type of opportunity, so I was grateful. There had been nothing left unsaid or undone between me and my father—nothing.

Dad was taken home by an ambulance. There were no sirens or lights. Before leaving the hospital, I called Bob Flood at Flood Oil to see if they could line the streets of Eden to pay a last tribute to Dad, but come to find out, the ambulance took the back roads home, so that didn't happen. Plus, Pop used to point out to us that the traffic jams in Eden could be brutal. That occurred when the Flood Oil truck and the mailman left town.

Dale and I helped him out of the wheelchair—we had to steady him. He was so weak. As we propped him up, his head was buried in Dale's shoulder. We gently laid him down on his bed. As difficult as it was to know that very soon Dad would no longer be with us, Charlene and I were extremely grateful we were allowed the opportunity to be there. We weren't complaining, believe me.

This was all a part of the Peanut Butter Promise process for my father, and it is all of ours at one time—hopefully later than sooner. Although we would be soon grieving Pop's death, no one was grieving his life. He hadn't been cheated. He lived hard, he lived well, and he had the opportunity to make a lot of things right before he died.

Word spread quickly that Dave Rose had come home to die, and with his time short, he received visits from some of his best friends: Earl Kehrmeyer, Gary Boyke, Dave Rahn, his first cousin Marv Grahl, and his fishing buddy Glenn Oestreich.

It was especially emotional watching Pop, who was ninety-two, say goodbye to his only sibling, his younger brother Victor, who was eighty-nine at the time.

"It's been a good run, Vic," Dad said, knowing that was it—at least, the last time he would ever see him on this side of heaven. You could feel the love between them. (Note: About seven months later, on May 14, 2020, Victor would join his big brother in heaven.)

During this time, my sister Gloria spoke to Dad by phone. A few precious moments came over the weekend when Dad's sons and the grandchildren visited. On Friday evening, Eric read a letter to his Grandpa as he was losing consciousness. On Saturday night, Eric's brother, Pastor Frank, prayed over Pop as he slept; by then, he was ever-so-slowly slipping away. Afterward, my brother Dale comforted Frank, letting him know it wasn't the first prayer Pop had slept through.

Sunday was the last day Pop was awake. I did have one last lighthearted conversation with him. As he lay peacefully with his eyes closed, I had some good news for him and Mom.

"Dad, as the commissioner of the Banana Peel Toss Association, I've done some figuring, and your pension would come to seventeen-and-a-half cents a day. Now, that is if and when you retire or die. Would you like me to file your retirement papers?"

Being an eternal optimist, he said, "Not yet."

He did catch the irony of that amount (that of his pension), which was the same amount he'd paid me per hour while I worked on the farm as a teen. He appreciated my attempt to bring humor into the moment.

As the gorgeous Sunday sun shined into the living room over him, Charlene "the caretaker" told him something that needed to be done.

"Pop? This is your pain-in-the-butt daughter-in-law."

He acknowledged her by opening his eyes just a bit.

"Pop, Steve, Dale, and I have to move you to your other side to keep fluid from building up in your lungs. It's going to hurt a bit. Do you still love me?" she asked playfully.

"You bet," he said cracking and mustering as much of a smile as he could.

That would be Dad's last words.

The rest of the day was peaceful. There was a time in the afternoon during the Packers and Cowboys game when it seemed Pop was leaving us. As a matter of fact, I even tried to tell him, "Dad, it's OK to go" but he would have nothing to do with that. I should have known that no one ever told David Rose what to do or where to go.

Honestly, it was really awful overnight into Monday. The following morning, October 7, I was in the kitchen when Charlene said, "Steve, you better come in here." Mother had just sat down to be by Dad's side. She spoke some difficult words to him.

"Darling, I'm here," she told her husband.

And what she said next through tears was not easy for us to hear, but necessary, at least for Pop.

Through tears she told him, "It is OK. You can go now."

And with that, Pop took four shallow breaths, and he was gone. It is amazing; experts will say how important it is for spouses and family to give permission to their loved ones to go, just like Char's Aunt Annie did the same for Uncle Maury about six months after Dad died. Like Mom and Dad, they'd had just celebrated seventy years of marriage when Maury passed. It's uncanny how that works.

As I gazed at Pop, he looked like he was sleeping. I picked up my cell phone so I might be able to get the time of death. On the face, it read: *7:07a.m., Mon., October 7*. As you probably know—the Peanut Butter Promise loves sevens, the number of perfection, and we got a few of them.

The sun from the east still beamed through the window onto Pop. His battle was over; there was a peace on his face. We should all be able to die in such a peaceful way. Mom, Dale, Charlene, and I shared our last quiet moments with him. It was strangely quiet after the oxygen was shut off, but he didn't need it anymore, and we were thanking God for that. We then called Hospice of Hope. When they arrived, they treated Father with such dignity. We prayed over him.

Then, it was time to call Uecker-Witt Funeral Home. About twenty minutes later, Lee Uecker and his associate John came in, gave their condolences, and spent a few minutes with us. They treated him with great care as they placed Dad on a gurney and carried him down the steps out the front door. From there, he was wheeled about fifteen feet to the waiting hearse for the trip to the funeral home.

From the deck of the house, alone, I watched as the hearse went down the driveway. It stopped, took a left, and then crawled down Highway W. In about seventeen seconds, Pop was out of sight. It was then that something occurred to me. *Dad had died in his own home, just the way he wanted, and that was because of Charlene, who, with God's help, kept her Peanut Butter Promise to help do that.* We miss Father terribly, but he'd had his wish fulfilled to die in his own home; there was never any guarantee of that—none of us have that. You don't have to read too many newspapers or watch too many newscasts to realize not everyone gets to do that.

As I write, it's nearly eleven months into taking care of Mom. We're having a great time. On Mondays, Wednesdays, Fridays, and Sundays, I make her eggs. On Tuesdays, Thursdays, and Saturdays, Charlene makes us oatmeal. We drink lots of coffee and keep things light. Mother loves the peacefulness of the deck, especially doing her crossword puzzles there in the summer morning sunshine. Like Father, it helps that she is passionately positive.

As of this writing, things are great. The bump in early 2020 was my health. As disclosed in the beginning of this chapter, a November 18, 2019, call from Dr. Atassi revealed I had prostate cancer. After consultation and prayer, Charlene and I decided that removing the prostate would be best. On February 7, 2020, Dr. Higgins removed it. The incontinence was everything they promised, and *that* is what landed me in Depends made by Kimberly-Clark. Last check, I'm cancer-free and living the dream of the Peanut Butter Promise with Charlene and Mom by my side. I can attest that it's easier to be humble when you're sixty years old and wearing an adult diaper, but this too shall pass.

Throughout this book, we've discussed in great detail the importance of DreamGoals. When Pop asked Charlene on August 7, exactly four months prior to his death, "Do you think I can make it to our seventieth wedding anniversary?" that was an important DreamGoal we all set. What were the odds he would not only make it to that day, but after nearly a year-and-a-half of daily banana peel tossing, he *would* live long enough for that celebration and that morning would be, unbeknownst to him or us, his last banana peel tossing?

Anniversary morning, he made the first, missed the next two, and hit the last two that went right into the middle of the target (our waste basket). He finished the year at .701, certainly the best in his division, right?

The point is setting our own DreamGoals and pursuing a plan of action can help. It's also important to understand there's a real joy in helping others achieve their DreamGoals and that is equally gratifying. The greatest example of that is what you just read, how Charlene, by the grace of God, was able to fulfill Pop's 2015 wish for her to help him die in his home. So along with your own DreamGoals, always be watching and listening for how you can help others fulfill theirs. As you do, you'll be helping others in ways more satisfying than you could ever imagine.

The Peanut Butter Promise has, and will continue to, help guide us through our daily challenges, and it can help you as well if you will let it. Charlene and I are living proof that there is quality life after mess-ups, that there can be peace and all kinds of prosperity, and you can have these things too as you passionately pursue the fulfillment of your purpose by being faithful to your calling. If you will, we're here to help you every step along the way, and as usual, we mean it.

That's a Peanut Butter Promise.

# ACKNOWLEDGMENTS

To my wife, Charlene, you are the most wonderful and loving person I have ever known. I have learned so many things from you about serving others. Without question, I am the most blessed man on the planet. I will continue to hold your hand and you closely, not only because I love you, but mainly so you can't get away from me!

To our dear trusted and loyal friend, Mike Utech. You always find a way to do everything we ask you to do. Without you, there would not only have been this book, but the others as well. Most admirably, you have found a way to patiently put up with me for over thirty years. Mike, saying thanks to you is not sufficient for all you have done for me, but thanks.

To our dear brother Dale, if there were words that we could find to express what you mean to us—we would share them, but we can't find them. So just know that your sister-in-love and I think that you are the best person that God ever created. No one deserves to be along for this ride as much as you—so enjoy it with us! And, oh, by the way, your 1.2 is coming soon.

To Dayton Kane, you are a great teammate and even better friend. Your positive attitude and perspective is contagious. Your abilities are amazing, and your availability has been so unselfish. You are one awesome person DK! And thanks for writing that letter to me in 2008 that started this wonderful relationship. I shudder to think if you hadn't.

To Michael Van Dyck, we want to say thank you for your dear and trusted friendship—and for your longsuffering much-needed help to bring this faith-building message of hope and encouragement of *The Peanut Butter Promise* to the world. You are a wonderful Brother. Charlene and I love you very much.

Special thanks to Craig Culver, Wayne Larrivee, Chester Marcol, Kevin Harlan, Dick Bennett, and Pat Williams for your trust and confidence in us, and the message of the Peanut Butter Promise. The well-timed arrival of all of you into Charlene and my lives epitomizes what Peanut Butter Promise Partners are about. God bless each of you.

To Justin Pierce and Simran Singh, we thank each of you for your love and help over the years. Justin, it was your phone call to me in 2007 that sparked the concept and the developing of the philosophy of the Peanut Butter Promise. Besides being a wonderful professional, you're one of the finest people on the planet. Simran, you're such a good friend, and example of the power of God's grace. We enjoy visiting with both of you when we come to Los Angeles.

To Ken Ruettgers, I thank you for all that you did for me beginning back in 1994 that led to writing *Leap of Faith: God Must Be a Packer Fan.* You are one of the most soft-hearted, humble teddy bears I have ever been blessed to be around. It's my fervent prayer that I can see you and Sheryl again soon, and introduce you to Charlene. You're a wonderful man, Ken.

Thanks to Austin Miller and Nena Madonia Oshman from Dupree Miller Agency for your part in helping to take this book from a Wish to a fulfilled DreamGoal. Also thanks to Deb Englander, Heather King, and all the great people at Post Hill Press who took this manuscript and brought it to life.

And the last shall be first...Charlene and I would like to give thanks to our Lord and Savior Jesus Christ. You gave us our lives so we could give life, hope, and encouragement to others. Thank you for forgiving and redeeming us into eternal life and making all of this possible. Your mercies are new every morning and we are grateful.

Amen.

# ABOUT THE AUTHOR

Steve Rose is a seven-time author, best known for his one-of-a-kind, feel-good book *Leap of Faith: God Must Be a Packer Fan*. It is historic in that it is the only book to ever combine a professional sports team and faith.

Over the past twenty-five years he has spent over 20,000 hours in research in the field of purpose, personal development, and potential. Currently he tries to spend at least two and a half hours daily in study, along with his wife, Charlene. This includes Bible study, devotionals, listening to educational and inspirational audio recordings, and watching inspirational DVDs and appropriate television.

Since 1996, Steve has presented his message of hope and encouragement to thousands of people, doing over two hundred Peanut

Butter Promise seminars, webinars, keynotes, and other presentations for groups, on campuses and for global-leading corporate brands that include: Kimberly-Clark, American Family Insurance, McDonalds, Oshkosh Truck Corporation, Postal Source, Wisconsin Milk Marketing Board, SEMEX, and The Salvation Army. One of his and Charlene's greatest passions is to speak to audiences.

He has also produced various television shows including the weekly *Leap of Faith* show that aired in 1998-99, as well as a thirteen-week national series called *Coincidence or Godincidence* in 2013. Along with Charlene he produced the powerful half-hour documentary *Only 16: Tragedy of 2 Billys* in 2017.

# CONNECT WITH STEVE AND CHARLENE ROSE!

Facebook.com/PeanutButterPromise

Twitter – @ThePeanutButterPromise1

Instagram – ThePeanutButterPromise

YouTube.com – Peanut Butter Promise

Email – Charlene@PeanutButterPromise.com

Be sure to check out the weekly inspirational *Peanut Butter Promise Power-Encouragement Podcast* on PodBean or wherever you get your podcasts!

If you would like to invite Steve and Charlene Rose to speak at your Company, Conference, Group or Campus Event, you may reach out to them at their official site at:

**PeanutButterPromise.com**